Motivating Struggling Learners

Every day, teachers face the challenge of motivating struggling learners. In this must-have book, bestselling author Barbara R. Blackburn shares how you can finally solve this problem and make your classroom a place where *all* students want to succeed.

You'll learn practical strategies for . . .

♦ understanding extrinsic and intrinsic motivation;
♦ building a trusting relationship with students;
♦ using praise and positive feedback effectively;
♦ empowering students and helping them own their learning;
♦ moving students toward a growth mindset;
♦ communicating high expectations for students;
♦ engaging all students in your lessons;
♦ scaffolding so all students will want to improve;
♦ helping students be resilient and not fear failure; and
♦ celebrating diverse groups of students.

Each chapter is filled with a variety of examples and tools that you can use immediately. Bonus: Many of the tools are also available as free eResources on our website, www.routledge.com/9781138792432, so you can easily download and print them for classroom use.

Dr. Barbara R. Blackburn is the bestselling author of 15 books and is a sought-after consultant. She was an award-winning professor at Winthrop University and has taught students of all ages. Barbara can be contacted through her website at www.barbarablackburnonline.com.

Motivating Struggling Learners

Learners

10 Ways to Build Student Success

Barbara R. Blackburn

Routledge
Taylor & Francis Group

NEW YORK AND LONDON

First published 2016
by Routledge
711 Third Avenue, New York, NY 10017

and by Routledge
2 Park Square, Milton Park, Abingdon, Oxon, OX14 4RN

Routledge is an imprint of the Taylor & Francis Group, an informa business

Library of Congress Cataloging-in-Publication Data
Blackburn, Barbara R., 1961–
    Motivating struggling learners : 10 ways to build student success /
by Barbara Blackburn.
        pages cm.
    Includes bibliographical references.
    1. Motivation in education—United States.   2. Learning disabled children—Education.   3. Children with disabilities—Education.   4. Academic achievement—United States.   I. Title.
    LB1065.B547 2015
    370.15'4—dc23
    2015004473

ISBN: 978-1-138-79242-5 (hbk)
ISBN: 978-1-138-79243-2 (pbk)
ISBN: 978-1-315-76210-4 (ebk)

Typeset in Palatino and Formata
by Apex CoVantage, LLC

Printed and bound in the United States of America by Sheridan Books, Inc. (a Sheridan Group Company).

Dedication

This book, my 15th, is dedicated to my late grandmother, Kate Blackburn.
She was and still is an inspiration to me.

Contents

Meet the Author

Dr. Barbara R. Blackburn has dedicated her life to raising the level of motivation, engagement, and rigor for professional educators and students alike. What differentiates Barbara's 15 books are her easily executable concrete examples based on decades of experience as a teacher, professor, and consultant. Barbara's dedication to education was inspired in her early years by her parents. Her father's doctorate and lifetime career as a professor taught her the importance of professional training. Her mother's career as school secretary shaped Barbara's appreciation of the effort all staff play in the education of every child.

Barbara has taught early childhood, elementary, middle, and high school students and has served as an educational consultant for three publishing companies. In addition to her teaching degrees, she holds a master's degree in school administration. She received her Ph.D. in Curriculum and Teaching from the University of North Carolina at Greensboro. In 2006, she received the award for Outstanding Junior Professor at Winthrop University. She left her position at the University of North Carolina at Charlotte to write and speak full-time.

In addition to speaking at state and national conferences, she also regularly presents workshops for teachers and administrators in elementary, middle, and high schools. Her workshops are lively and engaging and filled with practical information. Her most popular topics include:

♦ Motivating Struggling Students: 10 Ways to Build Student Success
♦ Instructional Strategies That Motivate Students
♦ Rigor Is NOT a Four-Letter Word
♦ Rigorous Schools and Classrooms: Leading the Way
♦ Motivation + Engagement + Rigor = Student Success
♦ Rigor for Students with Special Needs
♦ Content Literacy Strategies for the Young and the Restless
♦ Motivating Yourself and Others
♦ Engaging Instruction Leads to Higher Achievement
♦ High Expectations and Increased Support Lead to Success

Acknowledgments

To my wonderful husband, Pete, thank you for always being there for me and helping me do what I love.

Thank you to my parents—my Dad for being my first and best reader and editor and my Mom for supporting us both and providing delicious meals!

To the rest of my family, my stepson Hunter and my two sisters, Becky and Brenda, for your patience while I'm writing.

Abbigail, a special thank you. You are always an unbelievable sounding board.

To Lauren Davis, my editor, thank you for your ongoing support in order to help me be the best writer I can be.

To Peggy Presley, Nikki Mouton, Jill Morgan, Gererd Dixie, and Kate Sida-Nicholls—thanks for your suggestions, which helped me clarify and refine the content.

To John Maloney, thank you for a wonderful cover design.

To Julia Ter Maat and Apex CoVantage, thanks for the great jobs you did in copy editing and page make-up.

To my publisher, Routledge, thank you for giving me a wider audience for my books.

Finally, to the teachers and leaders in my workshops and all those who read my books and use the ideas to impact students, thank you. You make a difference every day in the lives of your students.

eResources

Many of the tools in this book can be downloaded and printed for classroom use. You can access these downloads by visiting the book product page on our website: www.routledge.com/9781138792432. Then click on the tab that says "eResources," and select the files. They will begin downloading to your computer.

Tool

Introduction

In this book, I return to the topic of my first book—student motivation. I've always wanted to write about it again because when I was a teacher, I grappled with motivating my learners, especially those who were struggling. I have taught all grade levels, and although I taught all levels of students, from gifted to those with specific learning needs, the majority of my teaching was with struggling learners.

In a recent report, *Engaging Students for Success: Findings from a National Survey*, the authors asked teachers for their perspective on a variety of topics. Several of their findings are pertinent to our topic of motivating struggling learners.

Findings

- ♦ 87% of educators believe that student engagement and motivation are "very important to student achievement." Engagement and motivation were ranked higher than teaching quality, parental support, or family background.
- ♦ 32% of educators strongly agreed that "I am good at engaging and motivating my students."
- ♦ 68% of educators strongly agreed that "engaging and motivating students is part of my job duties and responsibilities."
- ♦ 19% of educators strongly agreed that "I have adequate solutions and strategies to use when students aren't engaged or motivated."

Those numbers are striking. Although 87% of educators think motivation and engagement are very important, only 32% believe they are effective in those areas. That's the foundation of this book, to provide teachers assistance with motivation. I also address how engagement is related to motivation.

Throughout the book, we'll review key findings from research, with a practical eye on translating that research into strategies you can immediately use with your students. You'll hear stories of my own experiences (please note that all names of students have been changed) as well as examples from other teachers who have given me permission to share their accounts.

I hope you will find the information helpful with your struggling learners. I've given examples from a variety of grade levels and subject areas, but all of the ideas can be adapted to your specific classroom. View the material as a guide: something you can take and customize for your students.

As you read the book, please don't hesitate to contact me with questions. I love hearing from educators! You can reach me at bcgroup@gmail.com or through my website at www.barbarablackburnonline.com. Enjoy your reading!

1

Extrinsic and Intrinsic Motivation

Introduction

Do you teach students who are not motivated? The truth is, all students are motivated, just not necessarily by school. So let me rephrase my question. Do you teach students who are not motivated by learning? Of course you do!

What is the difference between a motivated and unmotivated learner? See if the following characteristics reflect your students:

High Motivation	*Low Motivation*
Shows interest	Lack of interest
Engaged	Disengaged
Focused	Distracted
Connected to teacher	Disconnected from teacher
Makes connections to other learning	Doesn't see relationships among aspects of learning
Safe and secure	Concerned about self-needs
Confident	Lacks assurance
Puts forth effort	Puts forth no effort
	May be bored or disruptive

Does that look familiar? Of course, the real issue is not identifying a student's motivation—it's understanding and dealing with it.

There are many considerations that impact motivation, especially low motivation, that we need to consider. These can be placed into three categories: personal factors, school influences, and outside issues.

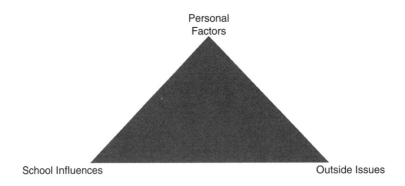

Personal Factors

School Influences   Outside Issues

Personal Factors

First, let's look at the personal factors that influence motivation. Students may have emotional or physical problems that impact motivation. One of my students struggled after his foster brother was tragically killed in a car accident. Jarod experienced severe nightmares, anxiety, and depression. Despite his best efforts at school, his motivation—and his learning—suffered.

Students may also have low self-confidence. This may be based on several things, including a lack of skills for the present learning activity or their past experiences in school. When students have a negative experience, that tends to snowball into self-defeating thoughts and behaviors. Often, these occurrences are caused by the absence of the necessary prior knowledge or skills needed to be successful.

Finally, students may have low interest in the subject, or they may not have a sense of trust or respect with the teacher. These present two different challenges, both of which we will address later in this book.

School-Based Factors

Besides personal factors, there are school- or classroom-based factors that impact motivation. For many students, the work they are asked to do is not at an appropriate level. If the assignment or activity is too easy, a student is bored. If it is too challenging, he or she may give up. We'll address solutions to this in Chapter 6: High Expectations.

I mentioned lack of interest as a student characteristic. This is linked to school when there is no real-life application of learning. Students need to see the connections between what they are working on and their lives. For a secondary student, this may mean connecting the subject with possible future jobs. For a primary student, it may be as simple as seeing his or her name in a math word problem.

A final demotivating school-based factor is the lack of perceived power by students. Think about that for a moment. I mentioned this to one teacher who responded, "I'm not giving power to my students; it's **my** classroom."

When students perceive they have no power, they lose motivation to be involved in learning. They struggle to gain some sense of control, at times in destructive clashes with their teacher.

A simple example is the lack of choice for students. If you ask students when they have choices in school, the majority will answer, "at lunch." Offering opportunities for students to build ownership through choices is one of the topics we'll look at in Chapter 4: Empowerment and Ownership.

Outside of School Factors

The final influencers on student motivation are outside ones, such as the attitude of parents, the educational levels of parents and families, the student's cultural environment and peers, and poverty. We know these have a tremendous impact on learning, yet we have no control over them. As teachers, we can attempt to shape parents' attitudes toward school and increase positive family involvement in learning, but we do not have direct control. The good news is that there are many examples of teachers and schools in which students have overcome these obstacles to become successful in school and life. In other words, you can make a difference, despite the challenges!

Maslow's Hierarchy of Needs

Before we finish our discussion of overall motivational characteristics, there is another framework to consider. Abraham Maslow (1943) identified a hierarchy of needs that people experience.

Maslow's Hierarchy
Self-Actualization
Esteem
Love/Belonging
Safety
Physiological

He proposed that before one can focus on the need for knowledge or understanding (self-actualization), the lower level needs, such as esteem, belonging, security, and survival must be met. For example, if I'm a student attending a new school, I care more about finding my classroom than I do about today's lesson. As you see, his work applies to student learning. Let's adapt his material a bit to consider at how this might look in a classroom.

Our goal is self-actualization, in which students focus on learning first. But notice all the other learning needs that must be met.

Needs Identified by Maslow	Application to Students
Aesthetic (Self-Actualization)	Do I focus on my own learning first?
Need for Understanding Need for Knowledge	Will I have the knowledge to be successful? What level of support will I have?
Esteem Needs Belonging Needs	Will I be successful? What will others think of me if I work hard?
Security Needs Survival Needs	What happens if I am unsuccessful? Do I have the knowledge and skills for success?

Extrinsic and Intrinsic Motivation

Now that we have some of the basics covered, let's talk about the two main types of motivation: extrinsic and intrinsic. Extrinsic motivation includes all the outside ways we try to influence a student, such as rewards, prizes, or grades. Intrinsic motivation comes from within the student. With extrinsic rewards, we can get temporary results, but for long-term impact, we need to help students activate their intrinsic motivation.

It's similar to looking at the ocean. I love watching the waves, but I'm only seeing the surface. I don't see the perilous undercurrents. Similarly, extrinsic motivation looks good, but we don't notice the dangers. Also, the true beauty of the ocean is underneath the surface. As we go deeper there are beautiful marine creatures, fish, and coral. Instead of short-lived waves, I can see long-lasting beauty. And that is intrinsic motivation.

Extrinsic Motivation

Extrinsic motivation is that which comes from outside a student: anything that is external. When I was a teacher, I used extrinsic rewards. I found they motivated my students, especially my struggling ones.

> **Examples of Extrinsic Rewards**
> Stickers
> Smiley-Faces
> Checkmarks
> Tokens
> Prizes
> Praise
> Numbers or Scores
> Grades

Positive Aspects of Extrinsic Motivation

Some authors, such as Alfie Kohn (2000), believe there are not any appropriate uses for external motivation. Based on my experiences, I believe there are limited uses for it. For example, I agree with Daniel Pink (2011), author of *Drive*, who compares extrinsic motivation to caffeine, noting it gets you going (although you are less motivated later). There were times that the only way I could get my struggling learners to begin a task was to promise a reward. It was effective, and oftentimes I could then move them beyond the initial reward.

Larry Ferlazzo in *Self-Driven Learning* (2013) also points out that everyone needs some baseline rewards, such as a clean classroom, a caring teacher, engaging lessons, and fair grading, in order to be motivated to learn. And Daniel Pink notes that extrinsic rewards do work for a short time for mechanical, rote tasks.

Negative Aspects of Extrinsic Motivation

There is, however, a downside to extrinsic motivation. It is temporary. To keep students motivated, you must continue to increase the reward. I read about a school district that wanted their students to read more. At the elementary level, students received a free book when they read a certain number of books. The reward proximity theory by Linda Gambrell (1996) notes that this is an effective use of rewards—to closely tie the "prize" to the activity, rather than using something like pizza to reward reading.

When the students moved to the intermediate and middle grades, however, books were no longer seen as a worthwhile prize. So the schools used small gift cards, such as iTunes or local restaurants (clearly, this district had more money than mine did). Of course, the problem was that by the time the students were in high school, that wasn't good enough. So at that level, their names were entered into a lottery for a car. Yes, a real car. I was both amazed and dismayed. How does this prepare students for the future? When they get a job or go to a college or university, they may not receive a prize for doing something they are supposed to do anyway!

The other side effect that the district didn't anticipate was the negative impact on intrinsic motivation. For students who did like to read, the prizes became a hoop to jump through, and in order to get the most points, and therefore prizes, they didn't necessarily read what they wanted to. In many cases, students opted for shorter, easier books.

A final negative aspect of extrinsic motivation that I saw with my students was that they began to see circumstances as out of their control. In other words, they didn't succeed because of their own efforts, but because of the prize. And that led to an attitude that if they were successful, it was because they were "lucky" or "I gave them the grade." If rewards are overused, students lose their internal strengths.

Negative Aspects of Extrinsic Motivation
Temporary
Constant Increase of Reward
Decreases Intrinsic Motivation
Lose Internal Strengths

Effective Ways to Use Extrinsic Motivation

"But," you may be thinking, "my students expect rewards. I can't just not use them!" So how can you effectively use extrinsic rewards? I think it's important to go back to Larry Ferlazzo's comments about baseline rewards and Maslow's hierarchy of needs. For all students, we need to provide:

- A clean, safe, caring environment;
- Engaging, interesting lessons;
- Appropriate support and scaffolding; and
- Clear and fair assessments.

In addition, when using extrinsic rewards, we should emphasize the feeling that accompanies the reward, reinforcing that the true reward is how you feel about your success. In other words, move from a reward to celebrating the learning experience.

There are three other specific tips for using extrinsic motivation. First, when using rewards, do so unannounced. Rather than saying "if then, then this," simply choose random times to reward students. By surprising students, they are encouraged to put forth effort all the time.

Next, reward students through affirmation of their work. Give them an authentic audience who can appreciate their quality learning. For example, rather than participating in a traditional science fair, use an "Invention Convention," and display their inventions for local community leaders.

Third, when you are using rewards, make them appropriate and meaningful to the student. Some students like stickers; others prefer tokens. It's also important to be respectful of the individual. Some students do not like to be singled out in front of their peers. If you know that, find another way to praise them: a note, an individual comment, or even a look. As teacher Suzanne Okey explains, "some students will appear not to respond positively to rewards, then it's necessary to figure out way to deliver rewards in a meaningful way to the student; give them a way to save face. In Chinese culture, saving face and losing face are huge concepts; it's big in our culture, too."

Intrinsic Motivation

Intrinsic motivation is that which comes from within the student. It is internal as opposed to external. With intrinsic motivation, students appreciate learning for its own sake. They enjoy learning and the feelings of accomplishment that accompany the activity. There are many benefits to intrinsic motivation. Students tend to earn higher grades, score higher on achievement tests, prefer challenging work, are more confident about their abilities, and retain information and concepts longer.

The Foundational Elements of Intrinsic Motivation

Intrinsic motivation has two foundational elements: People are more motivated when they value what they are doing and when they believe they have a chance for success. Students see value in a variety of ways, but the main three are relevance, activities, and relationships.

Value

Students typically see value through the relevance of the lesson. That's why we strive to show real-life applications when we are teaching. Sometimes relevance is how they might use the material in another lesson, at times it is the value for the future (college or university or the workforce), and for primary students, it's as simple as hearing their name in a story. In fact, most students have a streaming music station playing in their heads, WII-FM—what's in it for me? That's why they ask you, "Why do we need to learn this?"

When I do workshops with teachers, I know they come into my session with one burning question: "How can I use this information immediately?" Adult learners are juggling so many demands, they prioritize activities and their attention based on how well something meets their immediate needs. Students are similar, except they don't have the choice to leave. So often, we forget to show students why they need to know what we are teaching.

I was observing a student teacher when a student asked, "Why do we need to learn this?" It clearly flustered her, particularly because I was there to observe her, and she snapped back, "Because I said so." You can imagine the look on the student's face. The student teacher's answer ranks right up there with "Because we have to. It's on the test." Neither helps students understand why learning is important. Students are more engaged in learning when they see a useful connection to themselves.

Next, there is value in the type of learning activity you are doing. Students are generally more motivated by doing something, than by simple "sit and get." Charlene Haviland, a teacher in Norfolk, Virginia, has developed lessons that incorporate this concept. She uses the Harry Potter books to teach science concepts. For a discussion on the flying broomsticks used in the game of Quidditch, Haviland said, "We can even go into Bernoulli's principle and explore how we can take that from flying on a broom to . . . how airplanes work . . . and why some fly better than others." I don't know about you, but I'd sign up for that class quicker than I would a standard class on aerodynamics.

Finally, students find value in their relationships, with you and their peers. I heard a speaker say that the teacher-student relationship is foundational to everything else that happens in the classroom. I believe that is true. The old adage, "they don't care what you know until they know how much you care," is true. Students need to feel liked, cared for, and respected by their teachers. Many students also need the same from their peers. If they feel isolated from other classmates, they are disengaged and less likely to see value in what they are doing.

Success

Students are also motivated when they believe they have a chance to be successful. And that belief is built on four building blocks: level of challenge, experiences, encouragement, and views about success.

First, the degree of alignment between the difficulty of an activity and a student's skill level is a major factor in self-motivation. Imagine that you enjoy playing soccer, and you have the chance to compete in a local game. You will be playing against Lionel Messi (Argentina and Barcelona), named World Player of the Year four times in 6 years. How do you feel? In that situation, there's plenty of opportunity for challenge, probably too much challenge! Or perhaps you love reading novels, but the only language you can read is Russian. How motivated will you be in a literature class? For optimal motivation, the activity should be challenging but in balance with your ability to perform. That's a struggle for many teachers, but that is the foundation of our jobs—starting where a student is, then moving him or her up to increasing levels of difficulty and providing appropriate scaffolding for learning at increasing levels.

Just as we've discussed in many other areas, a student's experiences are an important factor. I'm more likely to believe I can be successful in science if I've been successful in other science activities. On the other hand, if I've had multiple negative experiences reading poetry, I'm less likely to want to read poetry, because I don't think I can.

A third building block to feelings of success is the encouragement a student receives from others. Encouragement is "the process of facilitating the development of a person's inner resources and courage toward positive movement" (Dinkmeyer & Losoncy, 1992, p.16).

When you encourage, you accept students as they are, so they will accept themselves. You value and reinforce attempts and efforts, and help the student realize that mistakes are learning tools. Encouragement says, "Try, and try again. You can do it. Go in your own direction, at your own pace. I believe in you." Encouragement can be in the form of words, but you can also provide encouragement through a consistent, positive presence in your students' lives. We'll delve more into this concept in Chapter 3: Praise and Positive Feedback.

It's also important for students to read and learn about people who failed before they succeeded, because the final building block is a student's views about success and failure. Many students see failure as the end rather than as an opportunity to learn before trying again. But there are countless examples, from Abraham Lincoln to Steve Jobs, of people who have experienced failure in their lives, only to become successful. How you define success and failure drives many of your beliefs about your own ability to succeed.

Strategies to Build Intrinsic Motivation

To build intrinsic motivation, there are basic strategies to use. We'll be exploring these in-depth in the upcoming chapters.

Strategies	Chapter
Have a positive, caring relationship with students	Chapter 2
Use positive reinforcement	Chapter 3
Empower and build ownership	Chapter 4
Develop a growth mindset	Chapter 5
Have high expectations for students	Chapter 6
Engage learners	Chapter 7
Provide support and scaffolding	Chapter 8
Build resilience	Chapter 9
Celebrate diverse groups of students	Chapter 10

There are also specific ways to deal with challenges related to building value and success.

For learners who struggle with . . .	Do this . . .
Seeing relevance	Develop real-life learning experiences and applications.
Not enjoying the activity	Attempt to involve the student more in the activity or provide an alternate activity.
Poor relationship with peers	Use care when assigning groups, design activities that build collaboration, pair student with a "coach" to help him or her assimilate into group work.
Poor relationship with teacher	Take time to build a more positive relationship with the student. Take it as your responsibility to improve the relationship.
Not feeling successful	Provide small chunks of tasks that students can complete successfully. Reinforce the successes.
Thinking they are not successful when they are.	Show them why they are successful. Positively reinforce the effort and achievement.
Thinking they are successful when they are not.	Reinforce that they have tried, but point out where they have made mistakes and provide coaching and support to help them succeed.

Source: Adapted from Opitz and Ford (2014), *Engaging Minds in the Classroom: The Surprising Power of Joy*

Conclusion

Students can be motivated for a variety of reasons, which can include personal factors, school influences, and outside issues. We can use extrinsic rewards to influence motivation, but they may only provide short-term results. A more effective strategy for working with struggling learners is to help them increase their intrinsic motivation. Throughout this book, we'll explore strategies that can have a positive impact on your students' learning.

Points to Ponder

Use the following sentence starters to reflect on the chapter.

I learned . . .
I'd like to try . . .
I need . . .
I'd like to share something from this chapter with . . .

2

Building a Relationship

Building a relationship with your struggling students is the foundation of helping them learn. Several years ago, my foster son was facing some challenges in school, which included clashes with several teachers. However, he had no problems with his reading teacher. When I asked him what made her different, he replied, "she likes and respects me." That's important to students. "But," you may be thinking, "I've tried with Jonathan, and nothing I do seems to work. He doesn't want to get along with me!"

Many years ago, my father was on a flight from Washington, DC, to New Orleans. He struck up a conversation with the gentleman next to him. At one point in the discussion, my dad asked, "What is the one thing you have learned in life?" The man responded, "I've learned that man can get along with other men if they try." At the end of the flight, he introduced himself—Martin Luther King, Sr. What a powerful statement. We can get along if we try, and sometimes we have to try for a long time.

My former professor, Dr. John Van Hoose, told of an experience with a school in Ohio. The faculty identified 40 struggling students who consistently underachieved and were in and out of the office for behavioral issues. Twenty teachers volunteered to work with them, and the program was organized simply. The teacher met with his or her two students for 5 minutes at the beginning of the day and 5 minutes at the end of the day. At the start of the day, the teacher asked, "How was your evening? Did you finish your homework last night? Do you have everything you need for school today?" At the end of the day, the teacher asked, "How was your day today? Do you have everything you need to take home to study? Is there anything going on I need to know about?" At the end of the first year, almost every student successfully completed the school year. A small number were suspended, but most of the students had improved behaviorally and academically. The time and effort invested was worth it.

Types of Relationships

There are actually two interrelated types of relationships you have with your students: a personal relationship and a learning relationship. Why do I differentiate? Because I've known teachers who had a great friendship with their students, but who didn't teach anything. They were very popular, but their students didn't learn. It's important to have that personal relationship, but it must transfer to learning. If you truly care about and want what's best for your students, you want them to learn!

Building a learning relationship means transferring that connection into a productive partnership aimed at improving the students' skills, both academic and social-emotional ones. You demonstrate this by providing respect through high expectations (Chapter 6) and caring by giving needed support (Chapter 8).

Teacher Characteristics

There are five characteristics of teachers who have good personal and learning relationships with their students.

Teacher Characteristics

Caring
Positive Attitude
Good Communicator
Knowledgeable Lifelong Learner
High Expectations

Caring

What does it mean to say you care? Everyone cares, right? If not, why are you a teacher? But there are a variety of specific ways to show that you care. For example, many teachers attend after-school events in which their students are participants. Or they talk to students about their personal lives and interests. It's also important to know how students learn best and to be responsive to their cultural needs.

One powerful way to do this is to have students write about themselves. High school teacher Sarah Ehrman explains,

> My first assignment is [to ask students to write an] autobiography. It must be three typed pages, anything about themselves. Everyone wants a chance to tell their story; where they were born, about their family. They can tell me "I have a bad home situation" or "I work long

hours." They write about a sport, extracurricular activities, anything they want. They are motivated when they think you want to know about them. When I started my first job, it was because the other teacher quit (it was an inner-city school teaching the "troubled" kids). They had 15 subs before I came, and they knew they were "bad kids." One of the students told other teachers [they] were so surprised that I cared enough to have them write 3 pages and that I cared enough to read it. I did not know that would be a big deal, but it was.

Another option is to ask students to create a timeline of experiences. After the students write their individual autobiographies, you can add photos (just take digital pictures and print them) and put them in a notebook to create a class book. It's a great way to encourage students to get to know each other better by reading the book. It's also a terrific tool for new students, parents, administrators, and substitute teachers.

Finally, a creative way to learn about your students is through the use of Culture Boxes. At the beginning of the year, ask your students to put 7–10 items that represent different aspects of who they are into a shoebox. Your students will love this activity, so get lots of boxes of varying sizes. As teacher Charlesetta Dawson explains,

> These objects reflect their family heritage, origins, ethnicity, language, religion, hobbies, and likes (foods, music, literature, movies, sports, etc.). The outsides of the boxes are decorated with pictures, symbols, and words/phrases to further explain who they are. Then the students share their culture boxes with the class. Every semester, my students always say that creating a culture box was their favorite activity because they got to be creative, share previously unknown information about themselves with their peers and teacher, and develop a better understanding of the similarities that we all have in common. The sharing might take more than one class period, but the time spent is well worth it!

Positive Attitude

Next, it's important to be positive. No one wants to be around someone who is negative all the time. One year, I was quite ill with the flu. Every time I recovered and came back to school, I picked the flu back up from my students. I missed three months of school, and when I returned, I still wasn't myself. One day, a student gave me a gift. It was a wooden pin with a chain connecting a second wooden square underneath. The top said "Teacher's Mood," and the bottom could be flipped from an A to an F. My student said, "you used to be an A, but since you came back, you've sort of been an F!" Students notice when we are sick or in a bad mood.

I'm not saying you have to be bubbly and giddy all the time. However, we can smile more than we frown, and phrase our comments in positive vs. negative ways, accompanied by a positive tone of voice and body language.

Examples of Negative vs. Positive Statements	
I can't believe you just did that! Will you just be quiet! Stop that! Really? (with rolled eyes, in response to an off-topic question) You are the worst class I've ever had!	That was a surprise. Let's take some time to settle down. Everyone please sit quietly at your desks. It's time to move on to something else. That's an interesting question. We'll explore it later. You are my most interesting class.

Good Communicator

Teachers with positive relationships with their students also are good communicators. Sometimes, we are so focused on our content we forget that *how* we teach it makes a difference.

Good communicators do several things. First, they state information and directions clearly. They also use visuals, such as anchor charts and graphic organizers to support the information. It's important to note that although visuals are an important tool, it's easy to overuse them. For example, when posting information or charts in your room, be sure you prioritize. Students can become confused when there are too many posters to look at.

When I was teaching, I regularly provided simple directions to my students, such as "turn to page 52 in your book." Immediately, there would be 12 hands raised, "What page did you say we were on?" I would repeat the directions, and then six hands would go up, "What page did you say we were on?" This would continue. I learned to write the page on the board, say it one time, repeat it once, and then point to the board. The visual supported my communication.

Another common way teachers use visuals is with PowerPoint slides or Prezi presentations. These can be effective, but too often we fill the screen with text and read the slide to students. We need to carefully plan the design of our slides, so they support rather than replace our communication.

> **Effective PowerPoint Slides**
> Have Only One or Two Key Points
> Have Plenty of White Space
> Have an Image to Support the Content
> Use Color, but Are not too Flashy;
> Use Charts, Tables, Video and Audio when Appropriate
> Sometimes Ask Questions

Good communicators also are <u>concise</u>, but provide necessary explanations. I remember one teacher when I was in high school. He spent hours explaining our content, most of which we didn't need to know. He went into great detail about facts and figures, but he really didn't explain the big concepts. Sometimes, we are so close to our subjects (and we love what we are teaching) that we can provide too much detail. Remember, students are beginners when they are learning, and we need to teach them what they need to learn with practical examples, not with minutiae. Concrete examples and practical applications are what help students remember facts and concepts. One of my most effective strategies was to tell stories about our topic, especially personal stories. You'll notice I do that throughout this book.

> **Characteristics of Effective Communicators**
> State Information Clearly
> Use Visuals to Support, but not Supplant Instruction
> Be Concise, While Still Providing Appropriate Information
> Provide Concrete Examples
> Apply Learning with Stories

Knowledgeable Lifelong Learner

It's also important to be knowledgeable about your subject. One year, I was assigned to teach sixth graders in an elementary school. I taught math, science, and social studies. Although I am certified as an elementary teacher (as well as a secondary one), most of my work was in reading/language arts. Math was also not my best subject in school. I was ill equipped to teach math to my students. I studied every night, just to be able to teach the next day. When they asked questions that moved beyond the information presented, I wasn't able to answer those questions. Needless to say, that wasn't my strongest year as a teacher. I didn't have the knowledge base to handle it.

We also need to have a depth of information about appropriate teaching strategies. One year, when I was teaching in a middle/secondary school, I was asked (told) to teach a photography course. This was before the digital age, when we were still using film. The former teacher gave me the course outline, and I discovered I was to teach the history of photography for 9 weeks before moving on to the practical, "how to develop film" portion of the class. This was totally out of my comfort zone. Again, I was studying the material, but this time, my strategic knowledge saved me. I chose to use the jigsaw method of teaching, in which students are placed in small groups, assigned a topic, move with other students assigned the same topic, research the information, then return to their original group as an expert to teach the material. Instead of me lecturing the whole time, students taught the material. In addition to being more engaging, students took ownership for their learning.

Jigsaw in 10 Easy Steps

1. Divide students into 5- or 6-person jigsaw groups. The groups should be diverse in terms of gender, ethnicity, race, and ability.
2. Appoint one student from each group as the leader. Initially, this person should be the most mature student in the group.
3. Divide the day's lesson into 5–6 segments. For example, if you want history students to learn about Eleanor Roosevelt, you might divide a short biography of her into stand-alone segments on: (1) Her childhood, (2) Her family life with Franklin and their children, (3) Her life after Franklin contracted polio, (4) Her work in the White House as First Lady, and (5) Her life and work after Franklin's death.
4. Assign each student to learn one segment, making sure students have direct access only to their own segment.
5. Give students time to read over their segment at least twice and become familiar with it. There is no need for them to memorize it.
6. Form temporary "expert groups" by having one student from each jigsaw group join other students assigned to the same segment. Give students in these expert groups time to discuss the main points of their segment and to rehearse the presentations they will make to their jigsaw group.
7. Bring the students back into their jigsaw groups.
8. Ask each student to present her or his segment to the group. Encourage others in the group to ask questions for clarification.
9. Float from group to group, observing the process. If any group is having trouble (e.g., a member is dominating or disruptive), make an appropriate intervention. Eventually, it's best for the group leader to handle this task. Leaders can be trained by whispering an instruction on how to intervene, until the leader gets the hang of it.
10. At the end of the session, give a quiz on the material so that students quickly come to realize that these sessions are not just fun and games but really count.

Source: www.jigsaw.org/#steps

It's critical that we know our subjects and teaching strategies, but we also need to be lifelong learners. Learning truly is forever. In both of the prior examples, I was as much a learner as I was a teacher. But it's also important to remember that education and teaching changes. In order to stay current, we must continue to learn. This is easy to see with technology. In our rapidly changing world, we must adapt to those changes. But there is also emerging information about effective teaching, and we need to stay up-to-date on that knowledge too.

Tools for Lifelong Learning
Professional Organizations
Professional Books
Professional Learning Communities
Conferences and Workshops
Twitter, Blogs, and Other Social Media Outlets

High Expectations

We will discuss high expectations in much more detail in Chapter 6, but let's take a look at it in the context of relationships with struggling students. One of the teachers I taught with in elementary school commented to me, "My students are struggling so much. I'm teaching easier concepts so they can feel successful." I know she had good intentions, but that isn't the best way to approach the problem. Realistically, when we "dumb down" our instruction, students know it. And what they also know is that means we don't think they can learn the standard material, and that means we don't respect them.

When students think we don't believe in them, they don't believe in themselves. When we think they can't do something, they will prove us right. But when we have high expectations *and* provide appropriate support, they can live up to the higher levels of learning. We have to find a balance, and we'll discuss appropriate leveling of material in Chapter 6.

High Expectations + Appropriate Support = Success

The Southern Regional Education Board (2004), developer of two highly respected school reform programs, *High Schools That Work* and *Making Middle Grades Work*, provide several other characteristics of classrooms that exhibit high expectations.

Implementing these 10 strategies ensures that the focus remains on learning.

Teacher Actions

Now let's turn our attention to teacher actions that support these characteristics. Actions back up the characteristics of teachers who build relationships with struggling students. We can group these actions into two categories: environmental factors and a focus on learning.

Environmental Factors

The overall environment in your classroom impacts your relationship with students, their motivation, and ultimately their learning. There are three specific ways you can improve the climate of your classroom: provide safety and security, encourage ownership of learning, and create a positive atmosphere.

Provide Safety and Security

First, students need a classroom in which they feel safe and secure. Until those needs are met, you won't make any progress in learning. What does safety and security look like in terms of what a teacher provides? In a word—predictability. Students need a set of rules and routines that are predictable so they know exactly what to expect.

One day, I rearranged my classroom. Alicia came in and was very upset, demanding to know where her seat was. As I showed it to her, she said, "That's not *my* seat!" She proceeded to walk around the room, looking under each chair, until she found one that had a scrap of tape underneath it. She then moved it to where I wanted her to sit. "*That's* my seat," she commented, and she was fine for the remainder of the day. We don't like to be surprised.

How many of you sit beside the same person every time you attend a faculty meeting or workshop? We like that comfort that comes with predictability just as much as our students do.

That's why we have discipline rules in our classrooms. They provide structure; students know guidelines for behavior, and they know the consequences of not following the rules. Students may complain about rules, but if you took them away, they wouldn't know what to do.

But there's also another way we make our classrooms predictable— through our instructional routines. These are the strategies and practices you use regularly to teach. For example, if you participated in one of my workshops, or saw me at a conference, or watched me teach graduate students, you would notice that I always use group activities. I believe in students working together to learn, therefore, I incorporate partner and small group activities in my instruction. My students came to expect it during each lesson. But what was important about it was that I also taught them what effective group work was. I didn't expect them to guess what they should do. I provided a clear set of expectations, allowed them time to participate in guided activities for practice, then moved them to independent work.

Other sample instructional routines include requiring students to listen, take notes, work independently, and complete alternative learning activities if they finish an assignment early. For each of these, it's important to teach them how to use the strategies you expect. It may seem basic, but many times, our students don't know these learning skills.

Sample Expectations for Effective Listening

Sit up straight.
Look at the teacher when you are not writing notes.
Draw or write examples that help you learn.
Pay attention.
Ask questions if you don't understand.

Encourage Ownership of Learning

Next, it's important to encourage students to own their learning. I remember a neighbor who didn't take very good care of her house and yard. One day, we were in the driveway talking, and she commented, "I like not having to take care of this. It's just a rental." Since she didn't own her house, she wasn't as invested in it. Sometimes our students feel the same way. They are renting space in our classroom, waiting for the year to be over.

We'll spend Chapter 4 discussing ownership and empowerment, but let me briefly provide an overview. Students are more vested in learning when they believe they have some control over the process. For example, asking students to write a report on a book or a person is a standard activity in schools. I know when I did that in school it was boring. When I was teaching, I gave my students choices. They were provided a list of options for showing they had either read the book or completed the research, and they could choose which one to complete. As a result, they felt like they were in charge of their own learning, and the final products were excellent.

Alternatives to Written Summaries	
Instead of reading a book and writing a summary . . .	Instead of researching a person and writing a report . . .
Create a video. Write a blog. Act out a scene. Write a song or a rap. Create a timeline and draw accompanying events. Invent a different ending.	Detail the number of things you have in common with the person. Create a fake Facebook page. Write a detailed obituary. Create a video montage of his or her life.

Create a Positive Atmosphere

Finally, it is important that the overall atmosphere is a positive one. We've already discussed the importance of our adult language, using positive phrases rather than negative ones. It's also critical to extend that to students. For example, in my classroom, students were quite sarcastic and critical of each other. I instituted a "no put-down zone." Anytime a student used a negative statement, effectively "putting down" another student, it violated our classroom respect rule. Although it took a few weeks, my students ultimately stopped making negative comments to each other. This made a big difference in learning, because students were no longer afraid to ask questions.

A related aspect of a positive environment is that your classroom is a bully-free zone. Bullying is a huge problem in our schools today, starting at the primary level. Although I had to confront some bullies in my classroom, it was nothing compared to today's world of cyber-bullying. We could spend an entire book just on this topic, but for our purposes, let's agree that bullying has no place in the classroom. Anne O'Brien (2011) provides tips for teachers to prevent bullying in your class.

Focus on Learning

Besides dealing with environmental issues, another action teachers can take is to focus on learning. This can occur in two ways: looking for the root cause of issues, and emphasizing progress as well as achievement.

Looking for the Cause, not Just the Effect

Are you interested in meeting students' learning needs? You have to probe deeper than surface actions to determine what is driving students to act the way they do. Do you want to solve a discipline problem? You have to deal with the cause, not the effect. Are you interested in being more successful with motivation? Then you have to suspend your prior beliefs about every student who walks into your classroom and ask, "Who are you, who do you want to be, how can I help you get there?"

Mr. Juarez told me about Mike, a student who showed no interest in reading. A discussion with other teachers brought up a variety of excuses—he's a boy, he doesn't know how to read, and so on. One day, Mr. Juarez told the class about a book he was reading in a graduate children's literature class and that he had read the same book when he was in elementary school. Mike was surprised that Mr. Juarez had ever read a book outside of those he read aloud to the class, and he expressed even more surprise that his teacher had a personal copy of the book. Mike said he didn't have any books. Mr. Juarez probed further and discovered there were no books in Mike's home. The only books available to Mike were those from the school.

By not jumping to conclusions, asking questions, and listening, he discovered that it wasn't that Mike couldn't read; he simply didn't know that reading was something you were supposed to do other than when you were told to do so in class. Mr. Juarez then decided to buy him a book to help him see that reading could be a great outside activity. After another conversation, Mike admitted to watching old western movies on television, so the teacher bought a book him a book about cowboys. He also met with Mike's grandmother, took them the public library to get a library card, and periodically asked Mike about reading. The result? Mr. Juarez found the real issue, and refocused the student on learning. Mike is now a solid grade-level reader who enjoys reading.

It's so easy to jump to conclusions. You have a test score; you have a record of discipline issues; you have an attitude that comes through every-day in your class. Some of your students may completely live up to that reputation. But other students could shine *if* the right person takes the time to listen, care, and help.

Focus on Progress in Addition to Achievement

Lastly, in addition to achievement, we should focus our and our students' attentions on progress. It's very easy to emphasize a final exam or achieve-ment test, to the exclusion of the small victories along the way. Struggling students in particular need to know they are being successful.

Students need to see progress to build a sense of confidence, which leads to a willingness to try something else, which in turn begins a cycle that leads to higher levels of success. Success leads to success, and the achievements of small goals are building blocks to larger goals.

We'll spend more time on this in Chapter 4: Empowerment and Owner-ship, and we'll also discuss the importance of a growth mindset in Chapter 5. When we focus on progress, and on the subsequent steps that build learning following that success, students are more apt to learn at higher levels.

Conclusion

Building a relationship with your students has an impact on learning. If you have a positive relationship, you'll see constructive results. If you have a negative relationship, you'll see corresponding outcomes. As you build both personal and learning relationships with your students, demonstrate the characteristics of a caring teacher, and take appropriate action to support the relationships, you will see a difference with your struggling learners.

Points to Ponder
Use the following sentence starters to reflect on the chapter.

I learned . . .
I'd like to try . . .
I need . . .
I'd like to share something from this chapter with . . .

3

Praise and Positive Feedback

Introduction

Praise is one type of extrinsic rewards, but one that most teachers find effective. I taught many students of all ages who appreciated my positive comments. Praise can make a difference, even when we don't personally or immediately see it. This story by Helice "Sparky" Bridges is the perfect example.

Who I Am Makes a Difference

A teacher in New York decided to honor all of her high school seniors by telling each of them how much of a difference they made. Using the *Who I Am Makes A Difference* Ceremony, she called each student to the front of the class, one at a time. First she told the class how that student made a difference to her. Then, she presented each of them with a *Who I Am Makes A Difference* Blue Ribbon.

Afterwards the teacher decided to do a class project to see what kind of impact acknowledgement would have on their community. She gave each of the students three more ribbons and instructed them to go out and spread this Blue Ribbon Ceremony. They were to follow up on the results, see who honored whom and report back to the class in about a week.

One of the boys in the class went to a junior executive in a nearby company and honored him for having helped him with his career planning. The boy gave him a Blue Ribbon, placing it on his shirt just above his heart. Then he gave the junior executive two extra ribbons, and said, "We're doing a class project on acknowledgement, and we'd like you to go out and find someone to honor. Give them this

---

(continued)

♦ 25

Blue Ribbon, then give them the extra Blue Ribbon so they can acknowledge another person to keep this acknowledgement ceremony going. Then, please report back to me and tell me what happened."

Later that day the junior executive went in to see his boss, who had been noted, by the way, as being kind of a grouchy fellow. He sat his boss down and told him that he deeply admired him for being a creative genius. The junior executive asked him if he would accept the gift of the Blue Ribbon and would he give him permission to put it on him. His surprised boss said, "Well, sure." The junior executive took the Blue Ribbon and placed it right on his boss's jacket above his heart. As he gave him the last extra ribbon, he said, "Would you do me a favor? Would you take this extra ribbon and pass it on by honoring someone else? The young boy who first gave me the ribbons is doing a project in school and we want to keep this recognition ceremony going to find out how it affects people."

That night the boss went home to his 14-year-old son and sat him down. He said, "The most incredible thing happened to me today. I was in my office and one of the junior executives came in and told me he admired me and gave me a Blue Ribbon for being a creative genius. Imagine. He thinks I'm a creative genius. Then he put this Blue Ribbon that says *Who I Am Makes A Difference* on my jacket above my heart. He gave me an extra ribbon and asked me to find someone else to honor. As I was driving home tonight, I started thinking about whom I would honor with this ribbon and I thought about you. I want to honor you.

"My days are really hectic and when I come home I don't pay a lot of attention to you. Sometimes I scream at you for not getting good enough grades in school or for your bedroom being a mess. But somehow tonight, I just wanted to sit here and, well, just let you know that you do make a difference to me. Besides your mother, you are the most important person in my life. You're a great kid and I love you!"

The startled boy started to sob and sob. He couldn't stop crying. His whole body shook. He got up, walked over to a drawer, opened it and took out a gun. Holding the gun in his hand, he looked up at his father and through his tears he said, "I was planning on committing suicide tomorrow, Dad, because I didn't think you loved me. Now I don't need to."

Source: http://youareadifferencemaker.com/BlueRibbonStory

Positive Aspects of Praise

Teachers have used praise in the classroom for many years, and almost every teacher I work with points to it as an effective motivator. I found that with my struggling students, they had heard very few positive comments about themselves; therefore they were particularly responsive to praise.

Praise can, if used appropriately, improve your relationship with students. Many come from negative or abusive homes, and you may be the only positive influence in their lives. Praise is a part of that positivity. Note that I said, "if used appropriately." We'll discuss that later in this chapter, but we do have to be careful not to use praise as a manipulator. If we do, that can actually damage our relationship to students.

Next, praise can balance criticism. McInnes (2011 as cited in Ferlazzo, 2013) states that it is necessary to have a ratio of three positive interactions for every critical one in order to develop and maintain a healthy team. I think we can apply this to students also. More often than not, students hear negative comments, both from their peers and us. And since brains are wired to remember negatives longer than positives, we must balance our comments. One suggestion is to sandwich criticism in between praise, so that's students do not become defeated.

Finally, praise can motivate students, particularly for the short-term. You've probably seen this in your classroom. You praise one student for something, and other students take note and follow. I taught students who simply did not know where to begin a task, or how to complete it, despite my instruction and scaffolding. They were overwhelmed. When I worked with them individually to complete the first step, praised the effort they showed, and then encouraged them to complete the next step on their own, they were more successful. I didn't overuse praise, but I did incorporate it as one of my motivational strategies.

Negative Aspects of Praise

Alfie Kohn, author of *Punished by Rewards*, is well-known as an opponent of praise and other rewards. It's important to consider his perspective as we discuss the use of praise in the classroom. He details five specific negative results of using praise with children and adolescents.

Negative Results of Praise
Manipulating Children
Creating Praise Junkies
Stealing a Child's Pleasure
Losing Interest
Reducing Achievement

First, Kohn believes that oftentimes, we are paying more attention to what we want from students, than we are with their well-being. For example, if we praise a student for good behavior, why are we doing that? Is it because we want them to continue those actions? If so, then how much are we manipulating them?

Next, praise, especially when it is excessive, can create praise junkies. Students can become overly dependent on us for praise. He also cites research results from Mary Budd Rowe at the University of Florida, in which students who were praised too much by their teachers were more tentative when responding to teachers' questions. For example, instead of stating an answer to a question, they answered with a questioning tone.

Third, Kohn points out that praise can steal a child's pleasure because we are telling him or her how to feel about what they have done. As he says about his daughter, "I want her to share her pleasure with me, not look to me for a verdict. I want her to exclaim, 'I did it!' (which she often does) instead of asking me uncertainly, 'Was that good?'"

Fourth, students can lose interest in what they are doing once praise is removed. I did see this with my students, especially those struggling to learn. They would continue to put forth effort as long as I was praising them and reinforcing the effort, but if I stopped, so did they. It's similar to other forms of extrinsic motivation—it works short-term, but may undermine intrinsic motivation for the task.

Finally, Kohn notes that praise can also reduce achievement. He shares that if students are praised for their work with a creative task, they tend to struggle with the next task. Additionally, when compared to students who were not praised at all, they do worse. This certainly has implications for us, given the high-stakes nature of education today.

In my experience, praise is an effective tool in the classroom, one that does motivate struggling students. I also found that praise boosted their confidence and helped them learn. However, it must be used effectively.

Strategies for Effective Use of Praise

Now that we've considered the benefits and criticisms of praise, let's discuss how to use praise effectively. Effective praise consists of six elements.

Effective PRAISE

Positive
Reinforces High Expectations
Appropriate
Independence Is Promoted
Sincere
Effort and Progress Are Noted

Positive

First, praise should always be positive. That may seem to be self-evident, but I've observed teachers who said they were praising students, but it was done in a sarcastic manner, with the corresponding body language. That undermines any positive effects of the praise. You may think sarcasm is an effective tool to use, particularly with older students. I respectfully disagree. My experience is that, although students won't show it, deep down sarcasm reinforces any negative comments they've heard in the past. Again, too often, they experience enough sarcasm at home and from their peers. They need us to be encouraging. Here are three examples of negative praise, with the positive alternative.

Negative Praise	*Positive Praise*
Finally, you did it. Well, thanks for getting started (sarcastic tone). Really, you finished?	I knew you could do it! That's a good start by chunking the information. Your effort really paid off—you finished the entire assignment.

Reinforces High Expectations

Next, praise should reinforce your high expectations. Notice I said high expectations. If we praise something that is too easy for students, we can actually undermine their confidence. As D. Stipek (n.d.) points out, "praise for successful performance on an easy task can be interpreted by a student as evidence that the teacher has a low perception of his or her ability. As a consequence, it can actually lower rather than enhance self-confidence."

In Chapter 6: High Expectations, we'll discuss what high expectations look like, but for now, it's important to realize that when we give students work that is too easy just so we can praise them, that isn't effective. Students are smart; they know exactly what we are doing when we lower our expectations. It means we don't respect them, and don't believe they can be successful. It is possible to have high expectations for struggling students and praise them for their successes, especially when we provide appropriate support (Chapter 8).

Appropriate

Praise should also be appropriate. This encompasses several specific behaviors we should use.

Appropriate Praise

May Be Public or Private
May Come in Different Forms
Focuses on What a Student Did, not Who the Student Is

First, praise may be public or private. There is mixed research, but typically, private praise is more effective, because it focuses on the student and his or her success, rather than how he or she looks in front of other students.

Next, praise may come in various forms. Some students simply need a smile from you. Others respond well to a written note they can keep and refer back to. Still others like to hear specific comments from you. The more specific you can be, the more effective the praise. When praise is too vague, the student doesn't know exactly what they did correctly. So no matter what form you use, be sure they know why you are praising them.

Reward certificates can be an effective way to praise students. You may want to praise effort or achievement. On the next page, you'll find three samples that you may want to use.

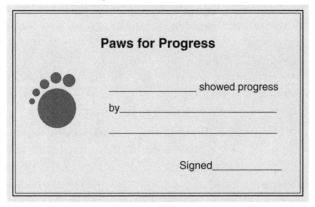

Paws for Progress

_____ showed progress

by_____

_____

Signed_____

Praise for a Peak Experience

_____ _____ excelled at

_____

_____

Signed_____

Lighting Up with Effort

_____ put forth effort

toward_____

_____

Signed_____

Students also react positively to a symbol. Karl Kosko, a former math teacher at Sullivan Middle School, found that his students responded to a new "member" of his classroom:

> I introduced Pythagoras the Goose [a stuffed animal who] loves math. He likes to watch people who are really working hard on math. So, if

a group of students is working hard he might land and watch them a while. However, if they stop working hard then he might get bored and fly off somewhere else. The reaction today was something one could see. A number of students decided they wanted the goose to come over at their table. Also, the table that ended up with the goose had some of the members encouraging others to keep working so the goose wouldn't "get bored."

Praise should also be about something a student did, not who the student is (we'll differentiate this a bit more later in this chapter when we talk about encouragement). Praise is effective when it is based on a specific action. For example, if a student successfully completed step one of a multi-step word problem, or predicted what would happen next in the story, that is more applicable than "you are a good student."

Independence Is Promoted

Next, praise should promote independence. If we aren't careful, students can become so attached to our praise that they can't do anything on their own. We don't want them to be more dependent on us; we want them to be less so.

This means that as part of our praise, we should ask questions of our students. For example, "how do you feel about your work?" Then we can agree with their positive comments. Or, "I notice you are very successful with that assignment. What did you do?" and then praise those steps. Questions such as these encourage self-reflection, and focus on the student's feelings rather than our own.

> ### *Questions That Promote Self-Reflection*
> What did you do to help you solve the problem?
> How did you figure that out?
> What would you do differently next time?
> How would you explain it to someone else?
> Why do you think you were successful?

Sincere

Effective praise is always sincere. In other words, it's not false praise, which students can identify in a moment. When we say "good job" and don't really mean it, or say it too often, it devalues praise and it undermines the trust students have with us.

Sincere praise comes from the heart. You mean it. It's authentic. And that comes through to students. It's also based in reality; it's not imagined. With sincere praise, you are identifying something specific the student has done or is doing, and that's what you praise. Whether you are praising a successful action, or their effort, students know and appreciate the reality of the praise.

When that happens, praise is meaningful to students. I remember Lauren, who was a very shy student. She wasn't confident about school, partially because her older sister was a straight-A student. Lauren thought she could never live up to that ideal. I had assigned a project for students to complete, and Lauren was very interested in the topic. She worked hard, and created a great poster presentation. I shared with her how proud I was that she had spent so much time and effort on the project, and that it had resulted in an A. What struck me was that she was more interested in my comments than in the grade. She became more confident, and continued to invest in future assignments.

Effort and Progress Are Noted

Finally, effective praise focuses on effort and progress rather than ability. Carol Dweck, in her book *Mindset*, provides research that supports this concept. She found that if students are praised for their ability ("you're so smart"), over time, their effort and achievement decreases. But, if students are praised for their effort ("I can tell you tried hard and successfully read the paragraph"), over time their effort increases, as does their achievement.

We'll discuss this at length in Chapter 5: Growth Mindset vs. Fixed Intelligence, but here it's important to consider how we phrase our praise. When my son was in the sixth grade, he struggled with math. My husband was always telling him how smart he was, and that he could be successful. Then, one day, my husband heard me speak on this topic. He changed how he talked with Hunter, encouraging his efforts to learn the material. By the end of the year, Hunter was quite successful and scored above average on the achievement test.

Our struggling students do need to hear that they can do the work. But a part of that is encouraging them to try, and reinforcing that effort.

Sample Praise Statements

Good, you noticed that mistake and fixed it.

I liked the way you tried to help yourself.

I can tell that you're really thinking about what you are reading.

I can see that you enjoy math. You have worked on these problems for over half an hour!

I really like how you used deductive reasoning to answer that question.

Encouragement

Many authors distinguish between praise and encouragement. Lavoie (2007) points out that praise is conditional; you receive it when you have done something. Encouragement, on the other hand, is unconditional and can be used even when a student is unsuccessful. It is not judgmental.

Years ago, I saw a cartoon that exemplified the difference between praise and encouragement. It showed a cartoon character fishing. In the first frame, the character caught a huge fish and others were congratulating him. That's praise. In the second frame, he caught a shoe. None of the bystanders spoke to him except one little boy, who said, "You did catch something. That's better than nothing. Are you going to try again?" That's encouragement.

Encouragement supports students and focuses on progress. You can do this through praise, but there is a different emphasis with encouragement. Rather than comparing a student to others or a set standard, encouragement values the student, not the performance.

What, then, is the difference between encouragement and praise? Lavoie (2007) provides examples for us.

Encouragement	Praise
You are a terrific student and I enjoy working with you. You make a real effort to participate in class. You seem to enjoy writing. You must have studied very hard for that test.	You're my best student. I like that you are always the first one to raise your hand. I'm so proud of your composition. Congratulations, you got the highest grade in the class.

Notice the difference between the two columns. The first focuses on the student and the process; the second on the achievement. While some may feel this is like splitting hairs, I do think Lavoie's point that we should be careful of conditional praise is accurate.

Conclusion

There are both benefits and drawbacks to using praise in the classroom. The key is to use praise effectively to help the student, not to manipulate behavior. Through positive, appropriate, sincere comments that reinforce high expectations and promote independence and effort, we can make a difference with our struggling students.

4

Empowerment and Ownership

Introduction

Empowering struggling students to take ownership of their learning is a key facet of motivating struggling learners. Consider a light bulb powered by electricity. In the classroom, empowerment "lights up" student ownership. Let's examine ways you can empower students, how teachers and students can create effective goals, and the characteristics of student ownership.

Empowerment

As teachers, we can take actions to empower our students. These include providing opportunities for choice, decision-making, scaffolding for independence, and leadership.

> ### *Empowerment Strategies*
> Choice
> Decision-Making
> Scaffolding for Independence
> Leadership

Choice

First, we can empower students by giving them choices. According to Keller (2012 in Ferlazzo, 2013), having the ability to choose our own focus makes us 5 times more committed to the outcome. If students are more invested in their work, they are more likely to learn.

We can provide choices in several ways: in what they learn, how they learn, and how they demonstrate learning. First, despite an era of standards and accountability, students can be given choices in what they learn. For example, if you are studying landforms or biomes in science, students could pick one to study, and then become "expert teachers" sharing their information with other students. This is a great alternative to you teaching all the landforms or biomes.

You can also allow struggling students to make choices about how they learn. In *Frames of Mind: The Theory of Multiple Intelligences* (1983), Howard Gardner proposed eight intelligences, or ways people learn most effectively.

Gardner's Multiple Intelligences	
Intelligence	*Learns Best Through . . .*
Linguistic	Words/language
Logical-Mathematical	Logic and/or numbers
Spatial	Visuals or pictures
Musical	Rhythms and/or music
Intrapersonal	Self-reflection and/or individually
Bodily-Kinesthetic	Physical activity
Interpersonal	Social interaction
Naturalist	Experiences in nature

Once you understand the different intelligences, you can use them to create activities that will enhance learning for your students. I met with a teacher who told me that this means that you should find out each student's type of intelligence, and then only teach him/her lessons in a way that matches that intelligence. I find that to be limiting, and unrealistic for today's classrooms. Instead, incorporating activities that address various intelligences allows students to construct deeper knowledge by seeing the concept through the different intelligence lenses.

For example, I may be a linguistic learner, but my knowledge of body systems is certainly enhanced through visuals (spatial). So, although you may want to provide instruction individually tailored to a student's intelligence(s), also plan lessons for all students that incorporate elements of the different intelligences. Inclusion of visual, audio, and digital texts in addition to print texts and an emphasis on collaboration with peers in small and larger groups are natural opportunities to address multiple intelligences.

A third option is to provide choices in how students demonstrate information. Kendra Alston, former Academic Facilitator at Kennedy Middle School, learned how important choices are when she was a student in a high school social studies class. She wasn't excited to study the 1920s and 1930s, but her teacher, Mr. Baldwin told them he was giving a *show me what you know* final exam.

> He didn't care how you showed it, as long as you showed what you knew. Things flashed before my eyes, but I was into theatre. So I researched the vaudeville circuit at the time and found Bessie Smith in theatre. She was a blues singer who sang in speakeasies; and I learned about the 20s and 30s through her eyes. On the day of the exam, I came in singing, stayed in character (others did essays, etc.). He asked questions and I answered based on what Bessie Smith would have said. It's the only way I got through it.

I liked using a Tic-Tac-Toe with my struggling students. For a particular unit or topic, I provided nine choices of activities they could use to demonstrate their understanding. They chose three to complete. You can also incorporate Bloom's Taxonomy or Webb's Depth of Knowledge into the assignments.

	Sample Tic-Tac-Toe: Fifth Grade	
Using what you know about the legislative system, choose one branch and convince the other two why it is most important.	Create a two voices poem comparing the United States government to one of the following: Canadian, Central American or Mexican government.	Create a graphic organizer using and comparing the branches of United States government.
Complete the web of political and social institutions on page 184 in order to analyze the two types of institutions.	Write a report about government in the United States. In your report, describe at least two ways local, state, and national government are alike and at least two ways they are different. Use specific examples to support your descriptions.	Create your own RAFT in which the topic is the Declaration of Independence.
Read the preamble to the United States' constitution. Explain why this document is important for American citizens, including at least three specific examples from the document.	Describe how a bill becomes a law to someone who just moved to the United States six months ago. Write your description in paragraph form.	Analyze the Federal System of Government using the graphic organizer on page 199.

I was recently in a primary school classroom. One of the teachers had a tic-tac-toe posted on the wall. The nine choices were "Things to Do When You Finish Your Work." The teacher shared that there were appropriate and inappropriate actions when you finish what you are working on. Then, she discussed options with her students, and together, they created the poster. That's a nice adaptation that incorporates choices and desired behaviors.

Decision-Making

Choices are one way to allow students to make decisions. However, it's important to actually teach decision-making and to give students opportunities to practice their skills. I used a decision chart with my students.

Decision Tree Template

Problem:					

Decision 1:		Decision 2:		Decision 3:	
PROS	CONS	PROS	CONS	PROS	CONS

Final decision and outcome:

Whether we were talking about behavior, or decisions made by a character in a story, a historical figure, or someone with a job, we would describe the choices as well as the pros and cons of each choice on the chart. Then, I asked students for their decisions.

I also provided opportunities for them to make decisions. For example, homework was always a struggle for my students. Many times, they simply didn't complete their homework, and most of the time they complained about it. One day, I began using two new strategies. First, I told them we were only going to have homework for three nights, and they could help me choose when that would happen. They immediately said they didn't want homework on the weekends. So then we discussed which nights they wanted homework, and they decided they wanted Mondays, Tuesdays, and Wednesdays, since it would give them four days off in a row.

Next, on the days when I assigned homework, I gave them two choices for the assignment. Both options accomplished my goal, whether that was reviewing material or previewing information. Students decided which they wanted to complete, and they were more vested in the work.

Scaffolding for Independence

Although we will address scaffolding in Chapter 8, I'd like to note a couple of points here. In order to motivate struggling students to succeed, we must provide appropriate support for learning. But that scaffolding should help students become independent, so they can learn on their own.

When I was a young girl, I wanted to ride a bike. However, I had to start with a tricycle. I needed to be close to the ground, and I needed the support of extra wheels. However, after a couple of years, I was ready to ride a children's bicycle. Of course, it had training wheels, because I still needed the balance of two additional wheels at the back. Next, I remember the day my father took off the training wheels so I could ride without them. He still held on to the back of the seat, to make sure I learned how to keep my balance without the extra wheels. Finally, he let go of the seat and let me ride by myself, one of the proudest days of my young life.

That's what we want scaffolding to be for our students. We want to provide more support as they begin to learn something then gradually lessen our backing so they become independent.

Leadership

Finally, we empower students when they are provided opportunities to be a leader. We do this all the time in primary classrooms—students are "line leaders," "book collectors," and "calendar counters." I always had a "teacher assistant of the day." My first year of teaching, I had a young lady who was an absolute nightmare to have in class. She rebelled against everything, and I was convinced she would be my downfall. One day, I asked her to be in charge of handing out papers. All of a sudden everything changed. She arrived to class early, handed out papers, and paid attention to everything I said. I overheard her tell another student that she was "Miss Blackburn's teaching assistant," so she had to behave in class. I was amazed, and realized how a simple request had completely changed her view of my class—she felt like it was hers, too, all because she had a leadership role.

As students age, however, we tend to provide fewer opportunities within the classroom for students to lead. Gin Sorrow shared a leadership strategy she used in her middle school/secondary classroom.

> I had some very social and unmotivated girls that were negative leaders in a class. I challenged them to teach the next section. They would come early in the mornings and work with me during planning times to prepare the lessons. It was a wonderful experience. I was able to see some of their methods for connecting with their peers that I could incorporate in to my teaching the rest of the year. The girls grew into more positive leaders and challenged the other students to improve. It is definitely a strategy I would use again.

Goal-Setting

Goal-setting is both a way to empower students (when we set goals for them) and for them to demonstrate ownership (when they set and track their own goals). There are five aspects to effective goals.

Effective Goals
Growth-Driven
Offer Structure
Attainable
Learning-Oriented
Specific

Growth-Driven

First, effective goals are growth-driven. In other words, they are focused on progress. For example, a growth-driven goal for a secondary student struggling with study skills might be: *To increase my understanding of content, demonstrated by a higher grade on my report card, by taking notes in class, annotating the notes, and reviewing them daily.* Although specific steps to achieve the goal are included, notice there is an emphasis on increasing understanding. Students need to see that progress is what is important, in addition to achieving certain benchmarks.

Offer Structure

Goals should also offer structure to students. Notice in the prior goal that the increased understanding will come from taking notes in class, annotating the notes, and reviewing them daily. Those are three detailed actions that are shown to increase comprehension. The structure also includes a time frame—these are actions to take daily. Finally, there is a guideline for success—demonstrated by a higher grade on the report card.

Attainable

Goals should also be attainable. One of my students wanted to set a goal that he would earn an A in all his classes. Prior to this, he had a D average. Although I wanted to have high expectations, I didn't want to set him up for failure. We agreed that the focus would be to improve his grade at least one letter grade in reading/language arts and in math, and that we would make similar goals for the other subjects during the next grading period. He reluctantly agreed and he agreed to concentrate additional effort in those two subjects. We also discussed exactly what he needed to do to achieve a higher grade, and I built in additional support (including learning packets he could work on at home) for him. The result? At the end of the grading period he earned a B in Math and a C in Reading/Language Arts. He was very proud, and his confidence soared. Over the year, he continued to work in all subjects, and ended the year with a B average.

Learning-Oriented

Larry Ferlazzo, in *Self-Driven Learning* (2013) points out there are two types of goals. Sometimes we set performance goals, such as "I'll make an A"; alternatively we set learning goals like "I'll read more challenging books." Although both are acceptable, learning goals provide more authenticity for students. Performance goals can actually narrow a student's focus and can impede progress when there is not a direct relationship between the goal and the outcome. For example, if my goal is to make an A and I study hard and only make a B, it can undermine my self-confidence.

Learning goals are far more effective. They provide opportunities for students to find creative ways to meet their goals, use problem-solving strategies, and focus on overall improvement rather than a single point in time.

Specific

Finally, goals must be specific. Sometimes, in our zeal to write goals that are attainable, we make them too broad. For example, *I will do better in class* may be a worthy goal, but how is it measured? What does it mean? Better in terms of behavior? Grades? We need to go back to some of our earlier examples and reframe it as: *During the next 2 weeks I will improve my behavior by staying in my seat and not interrupting my teacher when she is talking. I will improve my learning by completing my work on time, asking my teacher for help when I need it, finishing my homework, and staying after school for help on Thursdays.*

Goal-Setting in Action

One way I taught goal-setting was to have students create a "Me Poster" at the start of the year. I adapted this idea from one my dad used with teachers during workshops. I provided some starting points using basic pictures or shapes (see Components of *Me Poster*), and they could customize the posters. This gave me a tremendous amount of information about who they were and their interests and goals—probably more than I would have known if I had merely talked with them, or even asked them to write about themselves because many were reluctant writers.

Components of Me Poster

Star—In what way do you star as a student?

Trading Stamp—What part of your personality would you like to trade in?

Flower Pot—How can you make our classroom a better place to be?

First Prize Ribbon—For what one thing would you like to be remembered?

Crown—What is your crowning achievement?

Winner—Why are you a winner?

Turkey—What are the turkeys that get you down?

Question Mark—What one thing do you want others to know about you?

Arrow—What is one thing you want to accomplish this year?

I also like using vision letters, folders, and posters to help struggling students describe their goals. In a vision letter, students imagine it is the end of the school year (or grading period) and that, as they look backward, they discover being in x grade was their best year ever. They write a letter to a friend describing what made being in that grade so great, and by doing so, they define their vision for a good year.

You can adapt this with folders and posters. In these cases, students cut out or draw pictures or words and paste them on the poster to showcase their vision. If you choose to use a folder, you can use the panels to divide the year into four time periods, setting a vision for smaller intervals.

Ownership

Once you empower struggling students, they demonstrate three characteristics of ownership: self-efficacy, self-direction, and self-reflection.

Self-Efficacy

Self-efficacy is a person's belief in his or her ability to succeed. Students who have ownership in their learning typically have higher levels of self-efficacy. You see this through the confidence levels demonstrated by your students. Those with high levels of self-efficacy are more apt to tackle a challenging task, and they will persist longer even if they are struggling.

Self-efficacy can be impacted by several factors, including a student's past experiences, observing performance by other students, and verbal encouragement from others. There are specific actions we can take to build and reinforce positively a student's self-efficacy.

Encouraging Positive Self-Efficacy	
In order to impact . . .	*Try . . .*
Past Experiences	Having students keep a success journal recording their successful efforts. Focus their attention on times when they have successfully completed a task. Provide small, bite-sized tasks in which they can build a track record of success.
Observations of Other Students' Performances	Point out when a student is doing something well and explain why so everyone understands. Pair students together and provide opportunities for each to show his or her strengths. When a student makes a mistake, focus attention on the learning outcome, and how to prevent the same thing from occurring in the future.
Verbal Encouragement	Use appropriate praise to build self-efficacy. Use questioning strategies to help the student process his or her own learning. Be encouraging when a student stumbles.

Self-Direction

Next, students who have a feeling of ownership in learning are more self-directed than those who are not. They respond well when given choices, and are more apt to thrive when given multiple opportunities to learn. You'll find them suggesting ideas for extending the lesson, and asking their own questions about the content. Although they may still need scaffolding as they are learning new concepts, they will also make attempts to solve their own problems. Self-direction is interconnected with self-efficacy, as you will also see students taking on challenges and putting forth more focus and effort toward a task.

Self-Reflection

Finally, students demonstrate their ownership of learning through self-reflection. As you provide guidance and opportunities for them to self-assess, they will improve in their reflective skills. Since they are evaluating their own learning, it reinforces their ownership and their internal locus of control. Over time, they will look less to us for approval, as their own assessment becomes more accurate and important.

Exit slips are one of the most common ways for students to self-reflect. I used a simple three-question paper they completed as they finished the lesson.

Exit Slip
Today, I learned . . .
I can connect this to something else I know . . .
I still have a question about . . .

Another option is use student surveys, asking them to rank how they feel about their level of interest or about the level of difficulty in the lesson.

Student Interest	1- I can barely stay awake. 5- Highly riveting.
Lesson Difficulty	1- Way too easy. 5- Way too hard.

Source: Rollins (2014), *Learning in the Fast Lane*

Lindsay Grant and Christy Matkovich built in self-reflection as a part of their math classrooms. When each of them returned tests to their students, they gave them the opportunity to rework any missed items. However, in addition, they asked students to answer the following questions for each item missed.

Reworking Tests

Why I Missed the Question on the Original Test (circle one):

I didn't understand the question.

I thought I had it right.

I skipped a step.

I studied this but I forgot.

I had no clue about this.

I ran out of time or guessed.

I made a careless mistake.

Why I Know I Have the Right Answer Now:

By completing the additional information, students begin to think about why they missed the original question and how they can prevent that in the future. For example, if students are continually skipping a step, they will realize they need to slow down, take their time, and recheck their work.

Conclusion

Struggling students who feel ownership in their learning are more motivated and achieve at higher levels than students who do not feel a sense of investment in learning. As teachers, we can empower students by providing choices, opportunities for decision-making and leadership, and scaffolding for independence. As a result, our students will light up with self-efficacy, with self-direction, and through self-reflection.

Points to Ponder

Use the following sentence starters to reflect on the chapter.

I learned . . .

I'd like to try . . .

I need . . .

I'd like to share something from this chapter with . . .

5

Growth Mindset vs. Fixed Intelligence

Introduction

Have you ever seen a large oak tree? We had one in our yard when I was growing up, and I was always surprised at its size. But what really amazed me was to realize that huge tree started as a small acorn.

Our students are like that too. They will grow into a tree, but right now they may be acorns. And what will help them grow are our actions. Will we stand by and just assume that our students will always be acorns? Or can we see that they have the potential to be oak trees?

Fixed Mindset vs. Growth Mindset

That's the difference between a fixed mindset and a growth mindset. As Carol Dweck (2007) explains, a fixed mindset assumes that our character, intelligence, and creative ability are static and cannot be changed. A growth mindset, on the other hand, adopts the perspective that our intelligence, creativity, and character can change and grow over time.

These two views have a tremendous impact on teaching and learning. If a teacher believes in a fixed mindset, then he or she is saying there is no potential for growth. If a child is intelligent, he or she will continue to be so. If a child is struggling, it's because he or she just isn't "smart enough." On the other hand, if you believe in a growth mindset, you believe that students may start with a certain amount of ability, but that can change over time with effort and persistence.

For students, which of these they believe also matters. Students with a fixed mindset typically avoid challenges, feel threatened by others' successes, and give up easily. They want to look smart, and believe that working hard at a task means they are not smart.

Students with a growth mindset believe they can learn and become better. They embrace challenge, view effort as a positive part of learning, and persist through difficulties. Nigel Holmes provides a clear breakdown of the two mindsets discovered by Dr. Dweck. As you read the diagram, see if you can identify these traits in your struggling learners.

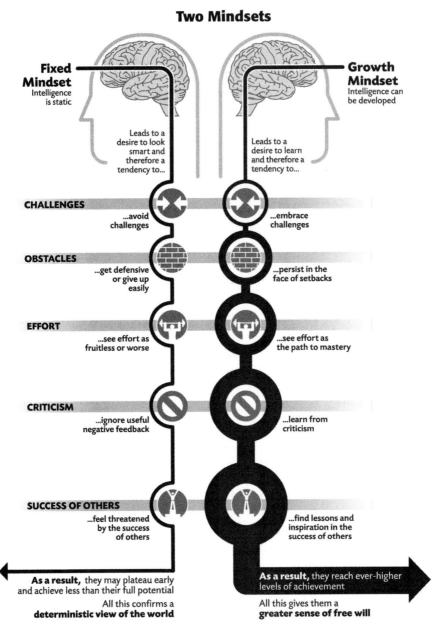

Two Mindsets

Fixed Mindset
Intelligence is static

Leads to a desire to look smart and therefore a tendency to...

Growth Mindset
Intelligence can be developed

Leads to a desire to learn and therefore a tendency to...

CHALLENGES
...avoid challenges
...embrace challenges

OBSTACLES
...get defensive or give up easily
...persist in the face of setbacks

EFFORT
...see effort as fruitless or worse
...see effort as the path to mastery

CRITICISM
...ignore useful negative feedback
...learn from criticism

SUCCESS OF OTHERS
...feel threatened by the success of others
...find lessons and inspiration in the success of others

As a result, they may plateau early and achieve less than their full potential

All this confirms a **deterministic view of the world**

As a result, they reach ever-higher levels of achievement

All this gives them a **greater sense of free will**

Source: By Professor Carol Dweck, graphic by Nigel Holmes. Used with permission.

Strategies to Develop a Growth Mindset in Your Classroom

A growth mindset is critical to a learning focused classroom. After all, if you don't believe a student can learn and grow, what difference can you make? During the remainder of the chapter, we'll look at six strategies to develop a growth mindset in your classroom.

Strategies to Develop a Growth Mindset in Your Classroom
Build a Learning-Oriented Mindset
Focus on Process as well as Product
Emphasize Mastery and Learning
Reinforce Effort
Decrease Learned Helplessness
Provide Multiple Opportunities for Success

Build a Learning-Oriented Mindset

First, we need to ensure that students have a learning-oriented mindset. Often, they don't. Most of my struggling learners had given up, believing they could never learn. I'll never forget Erika, who said, "Why are you bothering? Don't you know I'm stupid?"

We start the process by having this mindset ourselves, then constantly and consistently reinforcing it with students. We do this by providing the right support for them to learn (Chapter 8), encouraging them along the path (Chapter 3), and celebrating their resilience and success (Chapter 9).

Teachers can also ensure that all students are engaged in the learning process. Although we will discuss engagement strategies in Chapter 7, I want to share a specific questioning technique that is particularly effective for struggling learners. In *Engaging Students with Poverty in Mind*, Erik Jensen (2013) describes the difference between exclusive and inclusive questions. Particularly when we are activating prior knowledge, we ask questions to elicit students' experiences. However, at times, our questions may exclude struggling students, since they may not have a wide base of experiences.

Instead, use questions that are more inclusive. Take a look at the samples on the next page.

Exclusive vs. Inclusive Questions	
Exclusive	*Inclusive*
Who has ever traveled out of our city?	Who would like to travel somewhere different?
Who read a book outside of school lately?	I just read a book about xxx. Have you ever heard, read, or seen a movie about that?
Who completed their homework last night?	How many of you remember that we had homework last night? Can anyone tell me what it was about?
Raise your hand if you have been to an art museum.	Raise your hand if you've ever seen a picture you liked.

Source: Adapted from Jensen (2013), *Engaging Students with Poverty in Mind*

Using inclusive questions will help you engage your struggling students at a higher level, as well as helping them see they can contribute to the discussion.

Focus on Process as Well as Product

Another thing we can do to help students develop a growth mindset is to encourage them to focus on the *process* of learning, not just on the *product*. Many of my students just wanted to "get finished." They wanted to do their assignments quickly, and whether they were right or not didn't matter. After all, they weren't that smart anyway, right?

We need to help students slow down and focus on what they are learning and how they are learning. I used a three-step questioning process for students. With older students, they can use the questions for self-assessment; with younger ones, use the questions as verbal prompts.

Another way to focus on the process is during classroom discussions. Rather than asking a question, stating whether it is correct or not and moving on, use a roundabout model. For the first round, simply take all possible responses. For the second round, ask students to partner with another student and discuss the responses from the class. They should agree upon the best possible response. In the third round, discuss what the partners pick for the best answer and agree upon an answer. Finally, reflect on the process, with a focus on what helped students decide on the right answer. This takes a bit of time, so you don't need to do it every time you ask a question; just use it periodically.

Emphasize Mastery and Learning

Related to the focus on process is the strategy of emphasizing mastery and learning rather than grades. Particularly with older students, there is such a focus on "getting an A" that the joy of learning is lost. Or, students are so scared they won't make a good grade, they give up before they start.

Ames and Ames (1990) made an interesting discovery about two secondary school math teachers.

One teacher graded every homework assignment and counted homework as 30 percent of a student's final grade. The second teacher told students to spend a fixed amount of time on their homework (thirty minutes a night) and to bring questions to class about problems they could not complete. This teacher graded homework as satisfactory or unsatisfactory, gave students the opportunity to redo their assignments, and counted homework as 10 percent of their final grade.

Although homework was a smaller part of the course grade, this second teacher was more successful in motivating students to turn in their homework. In the first class, some students gave up rather than risk low evaluations of their abilities. In the second class, students were not risking their self-worth each time they did their homework but rather were attempting to learn. Mistakes were viewed as acceptable and something to learn from.

As a result, the researchers recommended de-emphasizing grading by eliminating systems of credit points. They pointed out there were positive results from assigning ungraded written work. They also suggested teachers stress the personal satisfaction of doing assignments and help students measure their progress.

Reinforce Effort

Encouraging and reinforcing effort are particularly critical for those students who do not understand the importance of their own efforts. In *Classroom Instruction That Works*, Marzano, Pickering, and Pollock (2001) make two important comments regarding students' views about effort.

Research-Based Generalizations about Effort
- ♦ Not all students realize the importance of believing in effort.
- ♦ Students can learn to change their beliefs to an emphasis on effort.

(Marzano et al., 2001, p. 50)

This is positive news for teachers. First, we're not imagining it—students don't realize they need to exert effort. And second, we can help them change that belief. Richard Curwin (2010) describes seven specific ways to encourage effort.

---

7 Ways to Encourage Effort
1. Never fail a student who tries, and never give the highest grades to one who doesn't.
2. Start with the positive.
3. See mistakes as learning opportunities, not failures.
4. Give do overs.
5. Give students the test before you start a unit.
6. Limit your corrections.
7. Do not compare students.

Researchers at Mindset Works© have created a rubric that assesses effort. The rubric categorizes students by Carol Dweck's mindsets, whether they are fixed, mixed, or growth.

Effective Effort Rubric			
	Fixed	Mixed	Growth
Taking on Challenges	You don't really take on challenges on your own. You feel that challenges are to be avoided. You prefer easy work.	You might take on challenges when you have some previous experience with success in that area.	You look forward to the next challenge and have long range plans for new challenges. If things are easy, you find them boring.
Learning from Mistakes	You see mistakes as failures, as proof that the task is beyond your reach. You may hide mistakes or lie about them.	You can accept mistakes as temporary setbacks, but you want to forget about them as much as possible. You don't use your mistakes to learn and improve the next time.	You see mistakes as temporary setbacks— something to be overcome. You think about what you learned from your mistakes and use it to do better at the task.
Accepting Feedback and Criticism	You feel threatened by feedback and may avoid it all together. Criticism and constructive feedback make you feel like giving up.	You may be motivated by feedback if it is not too critical or threatening. It depends on who is giving the feedback and how difficult the task is.	You look for feedback and criticism on your performance so that you can improve. You apply new strategies as a result of feedback.

(continued)

Practice and Applying Strategies	You do not like to practice and avoid it when you can. You do not have many strategies for accomplishing the learning goals or tasks, or the strategies you're using are not working.	You practice, but a big setback can make you want to quit. You are more willing to practice things you are already considered "good at." You are open to being given a strategy to meet a challenge, but you rarely apply your own strategies unless it is something you are already "good at."	You enjoy practicing and see it as part of the process of getting good at something. You may create your own practice or study plans. You use many strategies, think of some of your own strategies, and ask others about their strategies.
Perseverance (focus on task)	You have little persistence on learning goals and tasks. You tend to give up at the first sign of difficulty.	You may stick to it and persist if you get support from others. Unless others give you strategies for overcoming obstacles, you usually stop or give up.	You "stick to it" and keep working hard until the task is complete, even when it's difficult.
Asking Questions	You do not ask questions or do not know which questions to ask, but you can usually say you don't "get it" if asked.	You might ask questions about a portion of the task that you feel you can do. If you perceive it to be outside of your ability and skills, you probably won't ask questions.	You ask lots of specific questions of yourself and others. You don't just take things as they appear—you challenge yourself, the material, the

			task, and the teacher to make sure that you understand.
Taking Risks	You do not take risks, and if something is too hard you turn in blank work or copied work, if anything at all. You would rather not learn something than risk failing at it.	You will take risks if the task is already familiar to you. If not, you will resort to copying or turning in partially completed work. You may be willing to make a mistake to learn, but not if you are doing it in front of others.	You begin tasks confidently and you are willing to risk making errors. You'd rather try and fail than never try.

Finally, it's also important to revisit the concept of praise as it relates to effort. Erik Jensen (2013) shares:

According to Carol Dweck, author of *Mindset* (2007), the way a teacher talks to students greatly affects how students shape their mental models of their own capacity. Dweck points out that subtle conversations can actually change students' effort levels. Some well-meaning teachers inadvertently lower their students' engagement and subsequent achievement through what researchers call "comfort talk." These teachers think they are doing struggling students a favor when they say things like,

- ♦ It's all right. Maybe you're just one of those students who isn't good at math."
- ♦ Bless your heart, you really mean well.
- ♦ That's OK; you can be good at other things.

These well intended comments actually hurt students' performance (Rattan, Good, & Dweck, 2012). The lowered expectations, easily perceived by students—especially those living in poverty or other adverse circumstances—teachers need to be on a daily mission to build attitude, effort, capacity, and behavior. Don't make excuses or try to make students feel artificially better for doing poorly. Instead, focus on students' capacity to grow and change, and emphasize where they have control over their learning. Teachers influence student beliefs every day. Simple affirmations that steer students' thinking toward a learner's mind-set can have a lasting payoff.

(Jensen, 2013, pp. 83–84)

Decrease Learned Helplessness

Repeated failures and low achievement often lead struggling students to attribute their failures to internal causes and successes to external causes such as luck or ease of the task (Dweck & Elliott, 1983; Settle & Milich, 1999). Attributing success or failure to external sources is referred to as an external locus of control. Students with this attitude develop a learned helplessness over the years, knowing that they will fail, despite even good scores on tests and assignments.

Learned helplessness is a process of conditioning in which students seek help from others even when they have mastered information. See if this example sounds familiar:

A student is asked to solve a direct reading-comprehension problem, but he immediately raises his hand. When the teacher comes over, the student says he needs help. So the teacher reads the paragraph to the student and re-explains the question. The student still doesn't answer the question. Next, the teacher re-explains a regularly used comprehension strategy with the student. Finally, the teacher walks through the strategy and may even solve the problem for the student.

While this teacher's approach sounds justifiable, and maybe even familiar, the teacher is reinforcing the student's learned helplessness. This exchange undermines the student's independent ability to solve the problem. Other behaviors that continue a student's learned helplessness include an increased time of completion, lack of academic perseverance, refusal to initiate an attempt, and general off-task behavior. Thus, once a student has begun a run of learned helplessness, expect to see the behaviors repeatedly. In the scenario above, the student must learn to attend to the teacher's group instruction and attempt to solve problems.

Instead of rushing to the rescue of students who can succeed without us or even refusing to help such students, it is important to find ways to teach students to gain independence in their problem solving. In other words, find out why the student is behaving in a certain way, and plan a response that best builds academic success and independence. One way to help is to teach students how to learn and succeed without instantly making excuses and asking for help by following these steps.

Steps to Deal with Learned Helplessness

- ◆ Determine if learned helplessness exists.
- ◆ Explicitly model the preferred academic behavior.
- ◆ Teach the student a strategy for displaying the preferred academic behavior.
- ◆ Provide practice for the strategy.
- ◆ Set a cue to remind the student to initiate the strategy.
- ◆ Allow the student to succeed.
- ◆ Facilitate the student's problem-solving strategy.

Let's use the following scenario to discuss each step. In a middle/secondary history class, students are working desperately to understand a passage on George Washington. However, Annie hasn't yet begun the assignment. Instead, she rifles through papers and makes grunting sounds of exasperation. The teacher taps Annie's desk as she walks by. Annie rolls her eyes and waves her hand high in a frantic motion like one would make to catch a cab during a rainstorm. The teacher, however, ignores Annie and continues to work with small groups of students. Intermittently, she encourages students who are putting forth effort toward the difficult reading. Annie, irritated that she is being ignored, yells out, "You don't care about me!" (Note: What might look like an insensitive teacher to a passerby is actually a part of an organized effort by school personnel to help Annie overcome learned helplessness. In her IEP (Individualized Education Program), school personnel and Annie's mother agreed to ignore Annie's outbursts when she does not exert effort toward completion of a task.

A few minutes after Annie's outburst, Annie opens her book and begins to work. The teacher goes over to Annie, leans down, and praises Annie for attempting the assignment. She then reminds Annie that she cannot respond to her when she displays such outbursts, let alone when she does not show effort toward the assignment. The teacher also clarifies with Annie the expectation during independent practice. The teacher spends the next 5 minutes with Annie going over the passage so that she understands the information.

The teacher followed the learned helplessness plan as indicated:

1. Determine if learned helplessness exists.

The team already determined that Annie's behavior is purposeful and meant to avoid independent work in order to work with the teacher.

The behavior occurs in several classes when independent reading is assigned. Although Annie can now read near grade level, she spent several years below grade level and has learned to seek help even if she doesn't need it.

2. Explicitly model the preferred academic behavior.

Teachers have been asked to praise students in class who independently work on assignments. Annie has been asked to watch others' efforts in class to provide a model for what is expected of her.

3. Teach the student a strategy for displaying the preferred academic behavior.

Prior to this class, the special-education and general-education teachers have explained what is expected and how she can gain assistance. The first requirement to receiving help is to show effort for a minimum of 3 minutes. You may adjust this depending on the needs of the student. Then she will be allowed to ask the teacher for help. The number of minutes required for working independently is set to be increased by 1 minute each week.

4. Provide practice for the strategy.

Last week, Annie practiced the strategy of showing effort for 3 minutes. It was important that Annie understand what she should be doing as her replacement behavior.

5. Set a cue to remind the student to initiate the strategy.

The cue set by her teachers was a tap on her desk as the teacher walked by. The teacher would not stop by her desk to talk so as to minimize reinforcement for the behavior.

6. Allow the student to succeed.

The teacher did not give in to Annie's demand. Instead, she ignored the inappropriate behavior. When Annie showed 3 minutes of effort, she immediately went to help Annie for 5 minutes. The 5 minutes of help is Annie's incentive for working independently.

7. Facilitate the student's problem-solving strategy.

The teacher followed through with the plan and reminded Annie of the strategy. Overcoming learned helplessness, particularly at this time in her academic career, will be difficult for Annie. The teacher followed the steps appropriately but must remain consistent in her approach in order to help Annie perform more independently. Likewise, Annie's other teachers must remain as diligent. Following the same process can work for you, too. And the earlier we start helping students overcome this learned helplessness, the better off they are.

Provide Multiple Opportunities for Success

I believe strongly that students should have the opportunity to redo work they do not complete at a satisfactory level. Too often, struggling learners do what they consider their best work, yet it is unacceptable. At the primary grades, we use mastery learning, the concept that students continue to learn and demonstrate learning until we know they understand. If you are already doing this, I urge you to continue. But as students grow older, we tend to stop giving them multiple opportunities to show mastery.

The use of a "Not Yet" or "Incomplete" policy for projects and assignments shifts the emphasis to learning and allows students to revise and resubmit work until it is at an acceptable level. Requiring quality work, work that meets the teachers expectations, lets students know that the priority is learning, not simple completion of an assignment. It also encourages a growth mindset.

I had the opportunity to speak with Toni Eubank of the Southern Regional Education Board (SREB). As part of their comprehensive school reform model, SREB has long been a proponent of holding students to high expectations for completed work. She describes the model as Instant Credit Recovery for high school students.

This grading intervention practice requires that teachers rethink credit recovery completely. If it is okay for students to retake courses to meet standards, why is it not okay to retake tests that do not meet standards, revise essays, and redo classwork and homework that do not meet standards? Why do we let students "off the hook" for learning and for completing work that meets the standards during our classes, and then spend thousands and thousands of dollars requiring them to retake entire courses they have failed, many simply because they did not do homework? Instead of sitting in classes throughout the semester or year putting forth little to no effort, doing little work, failing tests or turning in garbage instead of high-quality work, students must now be required to work as they go. This method truly reflects job-embedded skills and habits and better prepares students for college and careers. Instead of retaking courses and earning credit (often for seat time only) in our current credit recovery programs, students must now work while they go—sort of a "pay as you go" method (Eubank, n.d., p. 1).

Eight Key Elements of the Instant Credit Recovery Model

1. Teachers no longer assign grades below a C.
2. Eliminate the use of zeros.
3. Late work is late, but it must be completed if teachers are to correctly determine if students know, understand, and are able to do whatever the verb within the standard calls for.
4. Students must be given extra help opportunities (required) to learn the information, skill, or concept to complete assignments.
5. Students must retake tests that they fail and redo all assignments they earn less than a C grade on.
6. Consequences change for students not having work ready to turn in on time.
7. Grading systems change from zeros or failing grades to "I's" or some other form of non-grade.
8. A few students will still fail no matter what. The goal is to get MORE students to complete MORE assignments and assessments to the proficient level of the standard.

In my university classroom, I used a grading policy with a three-part scale: A, B, and Not Yet. If my graduate students were unable to complete a project at an acceptable level (B or above), then they received a Not Yet and revised their work. Originally, my students thought that meant I was easier on grading. The first night, I usually heard someone say, "Wow, this means the worst I can do is a B. That is great." For those students whose work was not at an acceptable level, I required them to meet with me and come up with a plan for revising the work. Then I set a deadline for the revision. It's at that point that my students realized the policy wasn't easy—it was more challenging.

Since they were all teachers, it's usually one of those moments they learned more than content; they learned a process to use in their own classrooms. By the end of the semester, they had an entirely different attitude about learning and grading. As one of my students told me, "I didn't really like your Not Yet policy, but then I realized you were teaching us to focus on learning, not on a grade. I'm going to try to do the same thing with my students." When you require students to finish an assignment at an acceptable level, you show them you believe they can successfully complete the work.

Another alternative is to provide a structured opportunity to improve learning. Abbigail Armstrong, a former middle school teacher, now teaches undergraduate students at a local university. As she graded a set of tests, answers to one particular question jumped out at her. The students had made significant mistakes, and clearly did not understand the content. She realized that she had not covered the material as well as she thought. Rather than simply failing everyone in the class, she looked for an alternative to ensure understanding. As a part of their mid-term exam, she required her students to complete a question in a take-home testing format. Using any course materials, they had to revisit the prior test question and correct or clarify any incorrect or incomplete information. They also identified new information they believed they should have included in their original essays.

There was a key benefit of this process: her students viewed the tests differently. As one stated, "You didn't just give me a grade; if you had, I would just know that my answer is incorrect but I wouldn't do anything about it." Another pointed out, "We had to look up the incorrect information ourselves, so we will remember." Her students took ownership of their learning. And, rather than simply restating the question on the second test, she reframed it in a way that encouraged depth of understanding.

Conclusion

Students come to you with differing views of learning and intelligence. Some believe they are fixed, and can never improve. Others have a growth mindset, which considers intelligence and creativity as skills that can be improved upon over time and with effort. As teachers, we must decide which approach to facilitate with our struggling learners, and then take specific actions to support that mindset.

Points to Ponder
Use the following sentence starters to reflect on the chapter.

I learned . . .
I'd like to try . . .
I need . . .
I'd like to share something from this chapter with . . .

6

High Expectations

Introduction

T. D. Jakes, in his book, *Instinct*, tells the story of the giraffe and the turtle. Imagine yourself with your dreams and vision as the giraffe. You reach to the top of the tree and that is where you find your food. Imagine the turtle as all the people who have not understood your vision and tried to hold you back. The turtle finds his food on the ground. You both have different views of the world. As Jakes says, "We eat at the level of our vision."

Now, consider how this applies to motivating struggling students. Many of those students are like turtles—their view is low to the ground. They don't see the potential they would if they had a higher view of the landscape. We have to be giraffes—having the high expectations for our students, and then teaching them how to be giraffes too.

My best friend and I have a saying we share with each other when one of us is struggling. If she's going through a rough time, she knows I believe in her. But I'm quick to say, "I'm believing *for* you too!" At times, our students don't believe in themselves. We need to believe in them, for them, and help them believe for themselves.

In this chapter, we'll look at three specific areas related to high expectations. First, we'll consider the beliefs we hold and how they may be different than what we say. Then, we'll discuss how our beliefs translate into actions. Finally, we'll look at two specific instructional recommendations related to high expectations.

Beliefs

Our beliefs are the precursor to our actions. I have never met a teacher who said, "I have low expectations of my students." The problem is, sometimes we really do have low expectations, and we don't realize it.

How do you know if you have high expectations for your struggling students? Check out the list of high expectation vs. low expectation statements on the next page. Which ones have you thought or said about your struggling students?

High Expectation Statements	Low Expectation Statements
She can definitely do better, especially with my help. He didn't understand today, but I know he can get it! She tried her best, and if she continues to work hard, she'll get better. Even though he doesn't have support at home, he continues to do his best. I know she didn't do her best. I need to work with her so she'll know what to do next time.	He can't help it. She's done the best she can do. It really is okay. I know he's trying, but he just doesn't get it. Now that I've met her parents, I know why she's the way she is. It's really not his fault he didn't do well on the project. Maybe math just isn't her subject.

Low expectation beliefs can sneak into our consciousness. Let's examine the comment, "Now that I've met her parents, I know why she's the way she is." You may have laughed when you read that one. Haven't we all thought or said it about a struggling student? I did when I was teaching. A colleague chimed in, "Yes, the apple doesn't fall far from the tree, does it?" We may feel that way on the surface, but in reality, we are making a choice to write that student off as a lost cause. We're really saying this student can never accomplish more than her parents.

One of my friends heard Erik Jensen, who writes about learning and the brain, speak to this. He pointed out that "a student's DNA is not his or her destiny." He totally shifts the perspective to the potential for growth. Students are not necessarily locked into a future based on their family. Do you believe that?

You may be thinking, "Do our beliefs really matter?" Doug Reeves (2007) describes research in which teachers and administrators were asked what they felt was the biggest influence on student learning. In school where educators identified factors within their control, students showed 3 times greater achievement than in schools whose educators identified factors outside their control.

Factors Within Our Control	Factors Outside Our Control
Level of Instruction Reinforcement and Increase of Effort Support and Scaffolding Engagement Level of Classroom Activities	Poverty Parents' Educational Levels Parents' Interest Level Cultural Influences Community Influences Influences from Peers

When we focus on, or even blame outside factors for a student's poor performance, we are essentially giving up on a student. We're saying, "It's just sad. He comes from such a bad home life. There's nothing we can do about it." I don't know about you, but the reason I became a teacher was because I believe I can make a difference with all students. Let's not give up just because a student is struggling.

Thoughts such as these undermine our self-efficacy. We discussed this in the last chapter related to students, but we also have self-efficacy as teachers. This is our personal confidence level that we can make a difference with students. When we focus on factors over which we have no control, our self-efficacy is lowered. Teachers with a high self-efficacy believe there are specific things they can do that will positively impact learning for struggling students. They have a stronger sense of control and, therefore, take actions that support that belief.

How to Build Self-Efficacy

Make a list of times you have successfully helped a student overcome his or her struggles.

Reflect on and update the list regularly.

Keep a log of strategies that are successful with struggling learners and refer to it regularly.

Observe other teachers who are successful with struggling students.

Discuss strategies that help struggling learners with other teachers.

Share success stories.

Partner with another teacher to encourage each other.

Actions

On the other hand, our beliefs may not be the issue. We may have high expectations, but not translate those expectations into action. Our actions may inadvertently undermine high expectations, and students are quick to notice.

For example, Robert Marzano and others (2001) have found that when we have high expectations, we treat students differently. When questioning students, we call on them more often, ask more challenging questions, provide more wait time, and probe for additional information. How often do we use those strategies with struggling learners?

I know I made that mistake as a new teacher. Quinn struggled in my class, and nothing I did seemed to work. I ended up putting him in the last row of my classroom. As long as he behaved, I didn't call on him or push him to participate. Even though I said I expected all my students to learn, I didn't really show that to Quinn. And he understood my message. One day, we talked about his performance in my class, and he said, "Why should I try? You don't think I can do anything."

That was an eye-opener for me. I was so focused on making sure he behaved, I didn't challenge him. I was content to let him be a passive learner. My actions reflected subconscious low expectations.

Another year, I had a similar situation with Clarissa. She was bright, but lacked confidence. Her lack of self-efficacy caused her tremendous learning problems. She wasn't willing to try to learn anything new or challenging. I wanted to boost her confidence, so I provided easier work for her to complete. Instead of multi-step math problems, I gave her single-step problems. When we were reading, I allowed her to read easier books, many of which she had read before. I wanted her to feel successful.

What I didn't realize was that I wasn't doing my job. I wasn't teaching her to learn and grow—I was content to leave her in her comfort zone. By doing so, I also showed her I didn't think she could do any better. Once again, despite my comments to her that she could learn and that I had high expectations for her, my actions didn't reflect that.

Many researchers have detailed specific actions we take that are reflective of low expectations. I've used Robert Marzano's (2010) categories of our affective tone and our academic content interactions to provide a summary.

Actions That Reflect Low Expectations	
Affective Tone	*Academic Content Interactions*
Less eye contact Smile less Less physical contact More distance from student's seat Engage in less playful or light dialogue Use of comfort talk (That's ok, you can be good at other things) Display angry disposition	Call on less often Provide less wait time Ask less challenging questions Ask less specific questions Delve into answers less deeply Reward them for less rigorous responses Provide answers for students Use simpler modes of presentation and evaluation Do not insist that homework be turned in on time Use comments such as, "Wow, I'm surprised you answered correctly." Use less praise

The opposite is also true. When we have high expectations, we act in certain, converse ways. Which do you use with your struggling students?

Actions That Reflect High Expectations	
Affective Tone	*Academic Content Interactions*
More eye contact Smile more More physical contact Less distance from student's seat Engage in more playful or light dialogue Little use of comfort talk (That's ok, you can be good at other things)	Call on more often Provide more wait time Ask more challenging questions Ask more specific questions Delve into answers more deeply Reward them for more rigorous responses Use more complex modes of presentation and evaluation Insist that homework be turned in on times Use more praise

Instructional Recommendations

There are two additional recommendations I found effective for raising expectations for students. I learned to use both of these strategies over time, and they made a difference for my struggling learners.

> ### Raising Expectations for Students
> Clearly Communicate Expectations
> Use Appropriately Leveled Materials

Clearly Communicate Expectations

Our expectations should be clear to students. How can we expect them to be successful if they don't know what success looks like? I made my expectations clear using two main tools: modeling and rubrics.

Modeling

I modeled what I expected with my behavior, guidelines, and work samples. For example, when I wanted students to listen, I provided opportunities for them to share information while I listened attentively.

Another area my students struggled with was reading. Particularly in our science books, they would find a word they didn't know and simply stop. Then, they would ask for my help. I wanted them to be independent, so I taught them a set of rules for decoding and comprehending words in context.

What to Do When You Don't Know a Vocabulary Word
- Try to figure it out on your own.
- Read the sentence to understand the meaning.
- Look for prefixes or suffixes that you know to help you understand the word.
- Check to see if the word is in the glossary or margin of the book.
- Look it up on the internet.
- Use a thesaurus.
- Ask three other students for help.
- If nothing else works, ask the teacher.

I also modeled what I expected by providing samples of the work they were expected to complete. For example, if I wanted students to write an extended response to a question, rather than a few words, they needed to see exactly what I expected. This is particularly important, because many students think we want something different. For example, with a short answer, essay, extended response, students think we want length. Sometimes, they'll write down everything they know hoping we will pick out the part that is right.

Teachers want depth, some of which is determined by length, but is mostly determined by the quality of the answer. That can surprise students. So I showed them two or three examples of past students' responses, explaining what made those "good." Then, I paired students and gave them another sample. Together, they determined the quality of the work. Finally, each student wrote a response, and with a partner, they critiqued and provided recommendations for improvement.

Jill Yates follows this process in her art instruction:

> The most effective modeling that I have found has been in my use of examples and non-examples. Especially when I use this technique in art, the visible and concrete examples that are set before the students really help solidify what a desired and appropriate end product might look like. This is not to suggest that any of our products lack originality or creativity. Each is always unique. What I have found is that in the process of comparing two samples (an example and a non-example) and discussing and comparing the qualities of each, there remains no mystery in what is considered high quality and complete as a class. I tend to use my own stories and experiences,

plus student examples, to add high drama and humor within the task of comparing. I often start the year by comparing products extremely dissimilar in nature, and end the year comparing more subtle and/or equal products simply to encourage analysis, discussion, and higher-level thinking. I have found that in using examples and non-examples not only are standards met with more confidence, but rubrics are also created most naturally and quickly.

Rubrics

Jill's story is a great introduction to the second tool I used, rubrics. A rubric provides detailed descriptions of what you consider to be superior work, acceptable work, and unacceptable work for different categories of expectations.

Sample Expectation Categories for Rubrics

- Components to be Included
- Quality of Content
- Organization of Material
- Presentation of Material
- Grammar, Conventions, and Readability of Material

Ideally, students help you create a rubric, but I found that my students weren't ready for that, especially at the beginning of the year. I needed to provide rubrics, so they understood my expectations; then I shared partial rubrics, working with them to complete the categories; then we could create one together.

Effective rubrics have several characteristics. First, they are clear. When I create a rubric, I give it to my husband to read. If he can't understand it, neither will teachers or students. Next, you should see clear differences between your categories, whether they are grades (such as A, B, C, etc.) or categories (such as excellent, appropriate, needs work).

One lesson I learned as a teacher was to be careful how I graded. Was I grading based on the quality of work or something else? When I was a beginning teacher, I created rubrics that were oriented toward completion of the work, not the quality. That's a common mistake. If an "A" includes five examples, and a "B" includes four, etc., you're basing the grade on completing a task. What if my four examples are better than Shane's five examples? There's no differentiation for quality.

Rubrics can also be used for what you expect in terms of instructional behaviors. For example, I expected my students to work in small groups. They didn't always know what that meant. For some, it was "do my part and then let the others finish." Missy Miles created a sample rubric for effective group work for her students. You'll see one for older students, and one for younger children.

Cooperative Learning Rubric

	You're a Team Player!	You're Working on It . . .	You're Flying Solo
G Group dedication	The student is totally dedicated to his or her group, offering all of his or her attention by actively listening to peers and responding with ideas.	The student is partially dedicated to his or her group though sometimes becomes distracted by students or issues outside the group.	The student spends most of his or her time focusing on things outside the group; he or she is not available for discussion or group work.
R Responsibility	The student shares responsibility equally with other group members and accepts his or her role in the group.	The student takes on responsibility but does not completely fulfill his or her obligations.	The student either tries to take over the group and does not share responsibilities or takes no part at all in the group work assigned.
O Open communication	The student gives polite and constructive criticism to group members when necessary, welcomes feedback from peers, resolves conflict peacefully, and asks questions when a group goal is unclear.	The student gives criticism, though often in a blunt manner, reluctantly accepts criticism from peers, and may not resolve conflict peacefully all of the time.	The student is quick to point out the faults of other group members yet is unwilling to take any criticism in return; often, the student argues with peers rather than calmly coming to a consensus.
U Utilization of work time	The student is always on task, working with group members to achieve goals, objectives, and deadlines.	The student is on task most of the time but occasionally takes time off from working with the group.	The student does not pay attention to the task at hand and frustrates other group members because of his or her inability to complete work in a timely fashion.
P Participation	The student is observed sharing ideas, reporting research findings to the group, taking notes from other members, and offering assistance to his or her peers as needed.	The student sometimes shares ideas or reports findings openly but rarely takes notes from other group members.	This student does not openly share ideas or findings with the group, nor does he or she take notes on peers' ideas or findings.

Cooperative Learning Rubric (simplified version)

	You're a Team Player 3	You're Working on It . . . 2	You're the Lone Ranger 1	Total for Each Category
G Group Dedication	I listened respectfully to my teammates' ideas and offered suggestions that helped my group.	I did listen to ideas, but I didn't give suggestions.	I was distracted and more interested in the other groups than my group.	**Group Dedication** I circled number 3 2 1
R Responsibility	I eagerly accepted responsibility with my group and tried to do my part to help everyone in my group.	I accepted responsibility within my group without arguing.	I quarreled and did not accept roles given by my group.	**Responsibility** I circled number 3 2 1
O Open Communication	I listened to others' ideas and tried to solve conflicts peacefully.	I listened to others' ideas, but did not try to solve conflicts.	I was controlling and argumentative to my group.	**Open Communication** I circled number 3 2 1
U Use of Work Time	I was involved and engaged; I encouraged my group the entire time we were working.	I tried my best the entire time we were working.	I was not involved and did not offer any suggestions for the good of the group.	**Use of Work Time** I circled number 3 2 1
P Participation	I was a team member. I offered ideas, suggestions, and help for my group.	I participated in the project, but did not offer to help anyone.	I did not participate because I was not interested.	**Participation** I circled number 3 2 1
	Total			

Use Appropriately Leveled Materials

Vygotsky (1978) theorized that there is a zone of proximal development for learners. In other words, students sometimes do work that is too easy, or is in their comfort zone. Other times, they work at a level that is too challenging; therefore they are in a frustration level. In the zone of proximal development, students are working at the ideal learning level. Students may need a bit of help, or they may have to persist to be successful, but this is where they learn best.

Oftentimes, because we want students to be successful, we move them into materials that are in their comfort zone. One of the major areas for demonstrating high expectations is through the texts used during teaching. It's important for students to read a book or an article they can quickly and easily finish; those opportunities build self-confidence, provide enjoyable experiences, increase fluency, and may increase student motivation. But if that's all students read, they never learn how to deal with more challenging materials. We should consider providing text materials in all subject areas that are in a student's zone of proximal development.

Look for a balance: material should be difficult enough that students are learning something new, but not so hard that they give up. If you like to play tennis, you'll improve if you play against someone who is better than you. But if you play against Venus and Serena Williams, you'll learn less because you are overwhelmed by their advanced skill level. A good guideline is that for text to be appropriately challenging for growth, students should be able to understand about 75 percent of what they read. That percentage means students understand the majority of the material, while learning something new. One option for increasing text difficulty is to identify where your students are reading and provide text materials that match their level of growth.

Sometimes you must start with easier text in order to build to more complex text. One strategy for supporting students who are not reading at grade level is "layering meaning." If a student cannot read the grade-level or assigned text material, find another text on the same topic that is written at an easier level. Students read that selection first, and build their own prior knowledge and vocabulary; then they can go back and read the more complex text with your support.

Text difficulty should never be a limiting factor for students. I visited one school where students were never allowed to choose something to read unless it was "within their point range." That is not what I am recommending. Students always need the opportunity to read texts of their choice. And there are some books that may have a lower score on a readability scale, but the content is more difficult, perhaps due to the concepts described or the use of figurative language.

My point is that students need selected opportunities to read material that is at an appropriately challenging level. Please note the word *material*. Particularly with students who are reading substantially above or below their age or grade level, consider informational, nonfiction articles rather than novels or short stories. Graphic novels and technology-based materials are another useful option. These help address issues other than just text difficulty. Remember, I am talking about depth, not length; students shouldn't feel as if they are being punished.

When I was teaching, I used books that were labeled on grade level, but in reality, they were much easier than what students were expected to read on the state test or in real-life materials. That is still true today, and that is why it is important to use a measure that is consistent across all texts. There are a variety of readability formulas, which provide standards for text difficulty you can use to select texts.

Popular Readability Formulas	
Name of Formula	*Brief Description*
Fry	The most widely used of the readability formulas. The Fry is based on the assumption that the longer the sentence and the longer the word, the more difficult the passage.
Flesch-Kincaid	The Flesch-Kincaid is embedded in Microsoft Word programs and checks documents for the reading level of the passage.
Fountas and Pinnell Benchmark Assessment System	There are 26 levels in the Fountas and Pinnell System.
The Lexile Framework	The Lexile Framework is a computerized formula that analyzes entire text selections by sentence length and word frequency. It allows you to link difficulty of text materials with standardized tests. The website provides a searchable database of books, and many national and state tests also provide Lexile levels for students based on the test scores.

No matter which tool you use to determine the difficulty of text materials, remember that text difficulty is only one factor to consider when selecting text for or with your students. Other considerations include the appropriateness of the text for the students' age or developmental levels, the content of the material, and the purpose for reading, such as for interest or research.

Remember to always use your professional judgment when selecting text materials for your struggling students. Any readability formula should be the starting point for book selection, but it should never be the only factor considered. The goal is always to pick the right resource for the right reader at the right time. Remember to think about all aspects of the book or text and preview materials to ensure they are appropriate for your students.

Goldilocks' Rules

Another option you may find more student-friendly is Goldilocks' Rules, which includes the Five Finger Test. Lori Carter, author of the Book Nuts Reading Club, uses the parallel to Goldilocks to provide questions your students can ask themselves to determine if a book is too easy, too hard, or just right!

Too Easy	• Have you read this book many times before? • Do you understand the story very well without much effort? • Do you know and understand almost every word? • Can you read the book smoothly and fluently without much practice or effort?
Just Right	• Is this book new to you? • Do you understand most of the book? • Are there a few words per page that you don't recognize or know the meaning of instantly? Remember to use the Five Finger Test. • Can someone help you with the book if you hit a tough spot?
Too Hard	• Are there more than a few words on a page that you don't recognize or know the meaning of? Remember the Five Finger Test. • Are you confused about what is happening in most of the book? • When you read, are you struggling and does it sound choppy? • Is everyone busy and unable to help you if you hit a tough spot?

Source: www.booknutsreadingclub.com/goldilocksrule.html

Five Finger Test

1. First choose the book you think you would like to read.
2. Find a page of text somewhere in the middle of the book. Find a page with lots of text (words) and few or no pictures.
3. Begin to read the page. It is best to read the page aloud or in a whisper if possible while doing the test, so you can hear the places where you have difficulty.
3. Each time you come to a word you don't know, hold up one finger.
4. If you have all five fingers up before you get to the end of the page, wave the book good-bye. It is probably too difficult for you right now. Try it again later in the year. If you need help finding a book, ask your teacher or librarian.

Ultimately, what you want to do is balance the level of materials for your students. Too often, we lower the level of text for our struggling students, especially in the content areas such as science and social studies. A part of high expectations is providing text that is challenging for students, then balancing that challenge by providing the appropriate support and scaffolding so students can be successful.

Conclusion

We know that having high expectations is important for our students, particularly when their expectations for themselves are low. It's important that we examine our beliefs to ensure they do represent a view of success for our struggling students. Then, we must put our beliefs into action, showing students that we do believe they can learn at high levels. By changing our actions, clearly explaining our expectations, and providing opportunities for them to work in the zone of proximal development, we not only motivate our struggling learners, we help them achieve at higher levels.

Points to Ponder
Use the following sentence starters to reflect on the chapter.

I learned . . .
I'd like to try . . .
I need . . .
I'd like to share something from this chapter with . . .

7

Engagement

Introduction

Student engagement is interrelated with student motivation. I'm not sure a student can be engaged without being motivated, and I've never seen a motivated student who was disengaged. But what exactly is engagement? Is it simply a student completing a task?

Mihaly Csikszentmihaly (2004) describes the concept of flow, which is one way to look at engagement. When you are in a state of flow, you are totally immersed in the task at hand. You lose track of time, and experience strong feelings of satisfaction. Surely you've seen this with a student. They are so totally involved in what they are doing that you must interrupt them to move on.

Characteristics of Engagement

Eric Jensen (2013) points out there are four components that are present during student engagement:

1. The engaged student pays attention in the sense that he or she focuses on the tasks associated with the work being done;
2. The engaged student is committed. He or she voluntarily uses the resources under his or her control, such as time, attention, and effort, to support the activity;
3. The engaged student is persistent, sticking with the task despite difficulties; and
4. The engaged student finds meaning and value in the task.

Carolyn Chapman and Nicole Vagle in their book, *Motivating Students: 25 Strategies to Light the Fire of Engagement* (2011), provide more specific information to describe engaged students. You can use the table on the next page, which describes how students feel and what they do, as a checklist to determine the level of engagement of your students.

A Motivating, Engaging Classroom	
How Do Students Feel?	*What Are Students Doing?*
Excited	Problem-Solving
Respected	Processing
Challenged	Questioning
Stimulated	Discussing
Enthusiastic	Sharing
Content	Cooperating
Accepted	Collaborating
Energetic	Being Engaged
Safe	Planning
Positive	Producing
Upbeat	Learning
Cooperative	Showing Evidence of Learning
Confident	Thinking
Hopeful	Discussing, Asking Questions, and Posing Solutions to Problems
	Making Links and Connections to Their Learning
	Being Metacognitive, Reflecting on Their Learning, and Setting Goals for Their Next Steps

In each of the descriptions of engagement, everything is student-focused. You may be wondering if you can make a difference with student engagement. John Hattie and Gregory Yates, in *Visible Learning* (2008), point out that over 50 percent of the academic outcomes of students result from what the teacher does in the classroom.

For example, let's examine four typical behaviors you commonly see in the classroom. Struggling students may be engaged, detached, bored, or anxious. What specific steps can you take in each case to improve student engagement?

Typical Behaviors		
Characteristic	*What You See*	*What to Do*
Engaged	Involved and focused on learning	Monitor periodically and adjust if needed
Detached	Withdraws from lesson	Provide specific small steps and a strategy that requires involvement to get them started
Bored	Exhibits off-task behavior	Provide more challenge or relevance
Anxious	Exhibits agitation or off-task behavior	Provide more support and coaching

Principles of an Engaging Classroom

There are six principles teachers can use to create an engaging classroom. When used together, you can facilitate a classroom that is exciting and motivating to struggling students.

> **Six Principles to ENGAGE Struggling Students**
> Excite the Brain
> Nudge with Uncertainty
> Grow from Strengths
> Activate Understanding
> Group for Collaboration
> Elicit Involvement

Excite the Brain

First, it's important to excite the brain. This begins as soon as students walk into your classroom. Use brain-teasers to start your class. This can be as simple as showing three examples of a topic and asking students to figure out what it is, or as complex as asking students to create a package, describing the correct dimensions, that will hold exactly 62 M&Ms without wasted space. Your goal is for students to immediately start thinking.

I've been in classrooms where the opening activity is to copy the standard or objective that is written on the board. Copying is a rote task that does not get the brain moving, which is our goal. If you are required to use the standard, reframe it as a question. Ask students to copy the question; then brainstorm ideas for responding.

Once you've started by exciting the brain, you want to continue that process with additional activities interspersed throughout your lesson. The more activities struggling students are involved with, the more their brain is working.

For example, rather than simply reading a text and answering questions, Connie Forrester uses Grand Conversations with her primary grade students.

I would usually introduce this strategy in October during our unit of study on non-fiction. To introduce the strategy, I would ask the children if they knew what the word conversation meant. After some discussion, one child would usually come up with the fact that conversation is talking. I would go on to tell the children that Grand Conversations are one strategy that the big kids use when they talk about books. I would explain the ground rules to the children. You would be amazed how quickly the children catch on and how much they enjoy this strategy. They would beg to use it after we had read a book. However, I found Grand Conversations worked best when used after a non-fiction text.

Ground Rules for Grand Conversations

1. One person talks at a time.
2. When you respond to a classmate, you make a comment, ask a question, or make a connection. Your response must match the previous person's train of thought. For example, if we were having a conversation about a spider's habitat and the next child began discussing what he had for dinner last night, the first child could pick someone else.
3. No one raises his or her hands. I explain to the children that when people have conversations no one raises their hands. We would either toss a beach ball to the person to talk or the child would sit up very straight to be recognized.

That's very similar to the Paideia method of teaching, which uses seminars to discuss books or topics to foster critical thinking.

Five-Part Process for Using Paideia Seminars

1. First, reading activities ask students to observe and analyze the seminar text.
2. Then, the teacher offers instruction on strategies for effective communication, and participants set speaking and listening goals.
3. During the seminar, the teacher's questions provoke more complex thinking and articulate self-expression.
4. After the seminar, participants assess their progress toward speaking and listening goals.
5. Finally, writing assignments develop ideas that students began to explore during seminar, requiring more thorough analysis and clearer expression.

Notice how involved students are in the process. Although it is teacher facilitated with guiding questions, the students carry the conversation. Particularly with struggling students, the guiding questions are a key part of the seminar, in order to support the students through the process.

Sample Guiding Questions

Why do you think that?
What is an example of your point?
Is there evidence in the text? If so, where?
Would you explain that in more detail?
Who else agrees with that? Why?
How is that applicable to our lives?

In order to excite the brain, look for alternative, creative ways for students to learn. By doing so, you'll engage all your students—especially those who struggle—at a higher level.

Suggested Lesson Activities

Use Reader's Theatre instead of Round Robin Reading

Create a video game

Write a riddle or a rap to explain vocabulary concepts

Using given materials, create a model roller coaster (uses math and science concepts)

With a partner, use interactive writing (taking turns) to create a journal for a historical figure (which must be rooted in facts)

Instead of writing a paragraph summarizing or describing the topic, use RAFT (Role, Audience, Format, and Topic), such as taking on the role of talk show host to do an interview (format) about the history of the Aztec Indians (topic) for the TV audience (audience)

Nudge with Uncertainty

Next, students are more engaged when there is uncertainty. When they know all the answers, they are in a comfort zone and don't need to fully engage in the task. Therefore, while providing support for struggling students, we also want to give them an activity that requires them to think through alternatives.

Jessica Guidry, one of my former undergraduate students, designed an ecology unit for her science classroom that applies this principle. Her students were introduced to the unit with the following task:

> You are an ecologist from Rock Hill, South Carolina. Recently, members of the United Nations have come together and decided that they must eliminate one biome to make room for the world's growing human population. You and a group of your peers have decided to take a stand. You will each choose one biome to present to the United Nations in New York City this April. It is very important that you persuade the members of the UN to keep your chosen biome alive! The UN has asked that you write a persuasive essay to present to the audience. They also asked that you bring visuals and information about your references. You must be sure that you include how your biome benefits the world population. You need to include information about the habitats, populations, animals, plants, and food chains of your biome.

Throughout the unit, she integrated a variety of other open-ended projects, such as creating a flip book on their biome, participating in a debate, and creating food chains/webs in addition to the regular mix of lecture, guided discussion, and laboratory activities. However, since she began with the open-ended, authentic situation, her students were more engaged throughout the lessons. They were continually applying the lessons to their problem: convincing the UN to save their biome.

Another strategy for older students is to use SCAMPER. SCAMPER is a checklist of idea-spurring questions (Michalko, 2006).

SCAMPER
Substitute something
Combine it with something else
Adapt something to it
Modify or Magnify it
Put it to some other use
Eliminate something
Reverse or Rearrange it

Let's say you want students to describe the causes of a particular event. They write their basic response, then work through the SCAMPER steps to elaborate on their answer. For the final response, they revise their answer, including additional detail they discovered through the process.

For primary students, you might adapt a common classroom activity. When I was teaching first grade, it was typical for me to show a picture to prompt interest in the lesson. To add some uncertainty, simply cut your picture apart into puzzle pieces, and only show one or two pieces. Then ask students to figure out what the picture is by using the parts they can see. They become immediate problem-solvers.

A final way to include uncertainty in your lesson is to ask "what if" questions. This works no matter your subject area or grade level. Begin the lesson by posing a question, "What if we ran out of water? What would we do?" Throughout the lesson on the environment and global warming, students are looking for the answers. Or, "What if Hermione didn't help Harry Potter? What do you think would happen?"

Sample "What If" Questions
What if X (a famous person) tried to solve this problem?
What if we rearranged the numbers in the problem?
What if the story ended differently?
What if bees stopped pollinating?
What if no one had nuclear weapons?
What if there were only two primary colors?
What if Hamlet didn't die?

Grow from Strengths

A very important aspect of engaging struggling learners is to help them work and grow from their strengths. Too often, our struggling students focus on their weaknesses, or what they can't do. To engage them at higher levels, we want to provide activities that allow them to capitalize on their strengths.

For example, one year, I discovered that for many of my students, taking notes, whether from the book or from our discussion, was a challenge. They didn't know how to organize the information, and too often, I caught them drawing pictures rather than taking notes. One day, I introduced a new way of note-taking. I provided a form with the headings for our discussion. They wrote down key points in the second column, and then when we finished each part, they drew pictures or symbols to help them remember the information. Their note-taking skills improved tremendously, and over the year, I was able to help them identify the headings themselves. They became independent note-takers, building off their strengths.

Note-Taking Form		
Heading	*Notes*	*Drawing*

In Chapter 4: Empowerment and Ownership, we discussed the concept of multiple intelligences, that students have differing strengths in how they learn. As I said then, that doesn't mean we should individualize every lesson to match a student's intelligence, but it is important to consider how this helps us build from our students' strengths. That's really what I did with the note-taking—drawing and visuals helped them learn, so I incorporated it into my lesson strategy.

What types of multiple intelligences activities can be incorporated into your classroom to help your struggling students? Let's look at two examples. The first chart shows a variety of options to use in a primary/elementary reading classroom. The second shows cross-curricular activities for middle/secondary students.

Sample Primary/Elementary Literacy Activities
for Multiple Intelligences

Linguistic Participate in two character debates Use dialogue in reading and writing Play word puzzle games	**Logical-Mathematical** Create timelines of events Use Venn diagrams for comparison Play games to form words using dice with letters
Spatial Draw or build settings Create posters of grammar rules Write concrete poems	**Musical** Write and sing songs Associate rhythms with different characters Read and write tongue twisters
Intrapersonal Keep logs of silent reading Allow for self-assessment of strengths and challenges Read aloud to a stuffed animal	**Bodily-Kinesthetic** Role play story or act out spelling words Play Simon Says with word actions Make letters with clay, paint, or sand
Interpersonal Participate in choral reading or Reader's Theatre Hold mock talk shows Share writing through the Author's Chair or an "Open Mic" night at your classroom café	**Naturalist** Hold Read and Write Outside Days Go on a nature walk for a prewriting activity Create a natural habitat to demonstrate understanding of reading

Sample Cross-Curricular Multiple Intelligence Activities for Middle/Secondary Students	
Linguistic Debate an issue Use a Paideia Seminar Use small group discussions	**Logical-Mathematical** Describe sequences of events using timelines Create outlines Design a code
Spatial Create scale models Use pictures for note-taking Use graphic organizers such as mind maps	**Musical** Write songs from a specified time period Create music videos to demonstrate understanding Use rhythm to help memorize facts
Intrapersonal Keep a journal Write reflective essays Set personal goals and track progress	**Bodily-Kinesthetic** Role-play a scene from a story, a historical event, or a job interview Conduct experiments Participate in a scavenger hunt
Interpersonal Hold mock talk shows Work in cooperative groups Interview people	**Naturalist** Work outside on project Use visuals related to nature to apply information Research environmental aspects of a problem

Activate Understanding

Next, to appropriately engage struggling students, we should activate their understanding. This builds on their strengths, as we just discussed, and provides a transition to new learning.

One of the keys to helping students learn is to make sure they build a strong base for new information. Several summers ago, my friend's son built a stone garden in my yard. First, he put down a layer of stone, checked to see that it was level, and then added sand and gravel to make the ground under the stone was even so that the first row would completely level. It took him much longer to do the bottom row than the top three rows. He explained to me that if the foundation wasn't right, the entire garden wall would be flawed. This is also true with learning.

For our students, the foundation is the knowledge they already have about a topic. To effectively teach students something new, we need to know what they already know or think they know about a particular concept. In some instances, they have knowledge that is incorrect, and we need to address their misconceptions in a way that leads them to understand the concept correctly.

For example, I was observing one of my student teachers in a science classroom. As a part of a lesson on electricity, he asked the students if anyone knew what "grounded" meant. One student immediately blurted out, "I know. That's what happened to me when I made a bad grade last week. My mom wouldn't let me go out with my friends." Everyone laughed, because, to many students, that's exactly what grounded means. But it wasn't what the student teacher was looking for in the context of electricity.

It's critical to understand your students' prior knowledge. If teaching is helping students move from where they are to where they need to be, you must know where they are. Don't skip this part. Your success at helping your students connect what they already know to the new content will determine how well they will retain the new knowledge.

LINK Strategy

Kendra Alston uses LINK for her struggling students. After they complete the L column individually, her students turn to a partner and share their answers. Then, she leads a short class discussion, charting out what everyone in the class knows about the topic. As she works through the lesson, students finish by writing what they now know (K), and they tear that part off to turn in as they leave her class. This provides her immediate feedback as to what her students learned or didn't learn in class.

L	I	N	K
List everything you know	Inquire about what you want to know	Now we are going to take notes	What do you now know?

It's important to share students' responses with everyone, albeit it in a safe way that doesn't embarrass anyone. That's why I like her method. She starts by allowing each student to write an individual response, so everyone has an opportunity to think about what they know. As Kendra points out, if I'm a student,

> by sharing with a partner, I can feel "safer" in case I'm not right. In the whole class discussion, I'm sharing "our" answers (mine and my partner's), so I don't feel like I'm out on a limb by myself. You could even add another option of sharing with two groups of partners before you share with everyone. However, don't sacrifice the whole class discussion. We all learn more together, and it's a safe guess that someone in my class knows something I don't know. Listening to all responses and charting them out for everyone to see helps me build prior knowledge when I don't have much.

Sticky Notes

Missy Miles describes an alternative approach to assessing background knowledge:

> As students come into class I hand each of them their own sticky note (which they love). I have a question or other directions written on the board that ask the students to tell me what they know about the topic we are beginning that day in class. For example, "List five things you already know about William Shakespeare" or "What do you know about the Holocaust?" The students respond to the statement or question on their sticky notes and then place their notes on the board. After all students have responded, I read each of the sticky notes out loud, often times categorizing their responses into appropriate fields. By verbally acknowledging each sticky note, all students feel as though they have contributed to the "background knowledge board." More importantly, many students realize they know more about the topic than they first thought as they recognize other students' responses. I hear whispers in the class such as "Oh, yeah," or "I knew that!" It causes students to feel as though they can be successful at learning this subject because they already know something about it.

Let me make another important point before we leave the topic of background knowledge. Did you know there are actually two types of background knowledge, the prior knowledge a student has about the content you are teaching and the prior knowledge about the learning strategy you are using?

In other words, in addition to discovering what a student knows about countries, it's also important to understand how much they know about how to listen in class, or how to take notes, or how to work together in groups. Find out what they know, and teach the strategy as well as the content.

I like the idea to assess how they learn

Group for Collaboration

Another way to build student engagement is to group students for collaborative activities. It's much easier for students to disconnect from learning in a large group. When you are planning for group activities, consider the following questions.

Planning for Group Activities

What is the purpose of the group assignment?
What is each student supposed to learn?
What skills are to be developed?
How is this group work assignment related to the content?
What are students to produce?
What format(s) will be used for the final project?
What avenues of support are available to students?
What resources are needed?
Will each student work co-operatively with group members, each completing a separate piece of the project to be compiled at the end, or will they work collaboratively to produce a jointly researched and authored final project?

Source: Adapted from Graham Gibbs (1994), *Learning in Teams: A Student Manual*

As we just discussed, knowing how to work together for learning is a strategic, and you need to assess if your students understand how to work together in a group. If not, you'll need to teach them how by modeling and providing practice. The group work rubrics on page 72 are a helpful tool.

One way to promote collaborative learning is through the Question Matrix.

Question Matrix						
What Is	When Is	Where Is	Which Is	Who Is	Why Is	How Is
What Did	When Did	Where Did	Which Did	Who Did	Why Did	How Did
What Can	When Can	Where Can	Which Can	Who Can	Why Can	How Can
What Would	When Would	Where Would	Which Would	Who Would	Why Would	How Would
What Will	When Will	Where Will	Which Will	Who Will	Why Will	How Will
What Might	When Might	Where Might	Which Might	Who Might	Why Might	How Might

Source: Adapted from Wiederhold (1995), *Cooperative Learning and Higher Level Thinking: The Q-Matrix*

This grid crosses basic questions (who, what, when, where, why, and how) with verbs (is, did, can, would, will, and might) to create a matrix that addresses all levels of questioning. If you divide the grid into four quadrants, you'll notice the upper left addresses basic questions; and the closer you go to the bottom right, the higher the level of the question. I copy the grid on bright colors of card stock, cut the squares apart, and put a complete set in a plastic bag.

After my students have read a portion of text material, or when we are reviewing for a test, I put them in small groups and give each group a bag of cards. In turn, each student draws a card and has to finish the question. For example, if I draw the question card "how would," I might ask, "How would you react if you lived in a country that faced a famine?" Then, the rest of the small group must answer the question. I've done this with hundreds of teachers, and you can use these questions with almost any topic. The game requires that students collaborate for learning. It works particularly well in grades four and higher, but you can simplify the game for earlier grades by limiting the number of cards, or only using who, what, when, where, why, and how to prompt the questions.

Elicit Involvement

Finally, to engage students, elicit their involvement in learning. That's really what we've been talking about in all the previous strategies. Rather than "teaching at them," teach to and with them. As much as possible, shift the ownership to learning to the students as we discussed in Chapter 4.

Ways to Elicit Involvement from Students
Use Pair-Shares to Discuss and Apply Information
Use Small Groups for Activities and Discussions
Use Movement to Help Students Focus
Use Quick, Short Application Activities
Mix Types of Activities
Cut Down on Transitions

One specific way to elicit involvement is to capitalize on students' interests in technology. I've scattered some technology examples throughout the book, but let's focus on technology for a moment.

Of course, technology-based activities are always dependent on the resources you have. I've been in classrooms that are still limited to Power-Point or Prezi presentations. Some teachers use websites with class information and resources. Others are allowing their students to use their cell phones to respond to queries using software that collects the answers, or simply to text comments or questions to the teacher. It simply depends on what you have to work with.

There are a variety of technology-based activities you can use to motivate struggling learners, and new and engaging tools emerge every day. Some of my favorites right now include using video streaming for guest speakers, having students create blogs or video blogs to demonstrate understanding, using tablets or computers to play games that allow students to apply information, and using apps to interact with the teacher or other students.

Another effective way to use technology in the classroom is to conduct virtual field trips. In today's budget-conscious schools, this is particularly helpful. Imagine the activities you can integrate into the classroom with a virtual tour of the zoo with primary/elementary students.

However, it's important to remember that the field trip itself should not be the end result. Any tour should be linked to your standards, and the activities should result in increased learning related to your objectives. In the sample on the next page, a visit to the Louvre was linked to a study of Egyptian history in a middle school class. With adaptations of the assignments, it could easily be used in a high school art class.

The Louvre Visit

Today we are going to take an exciting trip to Paris, France! Your ticket is www.louvre.fr/en and your vehicle is your computer, tablet, or phone. Please read the instructions carefully so your trip is not wasted. I want you to have fun and learn something new in the process. We will have a round-table discussion on our magnificent trip on Friday. Have fun and I can't wait to hear about your adventure!

1. As your tour guide, I suggest you learn some information about the Louvre Museum because you begin your tour. Start at the *Collection and Louvre Palace* link. Read the information about the history of The Louvre. You are in Paris and you call home to talk to someone you love. Tell them about the Louvre's history in 3–5 sentences. Include why the museum was established and how it has been important to France.
2. Now you are ready to take your tour. Using the same link go to *Online Tours*. Choose the following tour: *Egyptian Antiquities*. Walk around on the floor to several areas. Spend 10 minutes learning how to navigate through the museum floor. Go to the help menu for ways to better navigate the tour.
3. Choose one sculpture from your tour. Analyze how it reflects the culture of Egypt.
4. Interpret the artwork. Communicate the artist's statement. Describe what you think the artist is trying to say through the work of art. Expound on the feeling conveyed by the artwork. Describe what the artwork means to you, and why. Explain what you feel is the artist's intended purpose for creating that particular work of art. Examine why the artist made the choices in technique, materials, and subject matter and how they relate to the intended purpose. Your narrative should be approximately one page.

Note: For more suggestions, visit www.wikihow.com/Critique-Artwork (the suggestions in number 4 are an excerpt from this site).

Ideas for Other Content Areas

Math: Students can plan the trip to the Louvre, look up the flight, and calculate the cost.

Social Studies: Plan what to take and how to pack, discuss how to prepare to visit the country, learn about Paris, and the French government. Also discuss the history of Egypt and the symbolism of the historical time period.

Language Arts: How did the authors and poets of Egypt impact the culture? Also teach about critiques and writing the analysis.

You can also use Wikis or other collaborative writing and social networking tools in your classroom. Elizabeth Edmondson, in her article *Wiki Literature Circles: Creating Digital Learning Communities* (2012), provides six options for using Wikis as a part of the learning process.

Six Ways to Use Wikis in the Classroom

- ◆ develop research projects and document ongoing student progress;
- ◆ build a collaborative class annotated bibliography on assigned readings;
- ◆ provide students with access to all instructor handouts;
- ◆ map concepts, brainstorm, and link relevant online resources;
- ◆ facilitate presentations, instead of PowerPoint or other traditional methods; and
- ◆ collaborate on group projects and documents rather than emailing the documents back and forth between group members.

Conclusion

Student engagement is one of the critical parts of student motivation. Struggling students in particular are often disengaged from the classroom and from learning. Recognizing the characteristics of engagement, and strategically crafting activities that excite the brain, prompt uncertainty, build on strengths, activate understanding, facilitate collaboration, and prompt involvement not only motivates struggling learners, it helps them grow.

Points to Ponder

Use the following sentence starters to reflect on the chapter.

I learned . . .
I'd like to try . . .
I need . . .
I'd like to share something from this chapter with . . .

8

Scaffolding for Success

Another key to motivating struggling learners is to provide them with support and scaffolding. Consider a time when you tried to accomplish something new. For example, think about your first year of teaching. Did you need help or guidance? That's exactly how our students are as they move to higher levels of learning. However, you will want to provide different levels of support at different times, gradually moving them to independence.

Gradual Release

It's important to realize that support should be used at an appropriate level through the learning process. At the beginning of new learning, more support is needed. However, as the learning continues, we want students to become more independent in their learning. This is called gradual release.

One way to think about scaffolding is with a diamond, or rhombus. As you can see from the figure, it starts with "me" (meaning the teacher). The teacher begins by modeling a lesson. Next, we go to "us." There are two parts of this. First is the teacher and the students ("us") following guided practice. The second part of guided practice is "us," meaning students working with partners or in small groups. Finally, the student ("you") does the work independently.

How do you decide when to move a student through the various stages of gradual release? I wish I could give you a set formula, but there isn't one. Sometimes students need to see you model something once; other students may need multiple explanations and models. The same is true for the guided practice. Be sure you are observing their work and using formative assessment strategies to help you know when they are ready to work on their own.

Me, Us, You Diamond

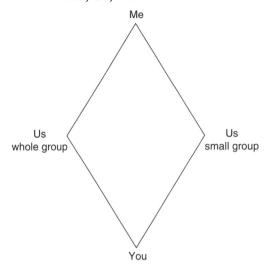

Strategies for Effective Support

There are a variety of strategies you can use to support students. We'll look at examples grouped around seven principles of effective support.

> ### *Effective SUPPORT*
> Structured
> Understanding is the Result
> Provides for Differentiation
> Promotes Connections
> Optimizes Strategic Learning
> Repetitionless
> Tied to Memory

Structured

First, effective support is structured. There is a plan to monitor student learning and provide extra help. One of the teachers I worked with told me, "I don't need to plan. When students need extra help, I'll know it." I find that not to be true. Prior to any instruction, we should consider possible stumbling blocks for students. When might they be confused? Is there prior knowledge they may lack? Or, is this something totally new that will need strong scaffolding?

For example, even if you know they will need visual support or chunking, don't just take that for granted. Plan how you will provide visuals and how you will chunk the information. Elaine McEwan-Adkins gives us an example for summarizing information. She suggests using five "Cs."

The C	What to Do	My Notes
Comprehend	Read and understand the text.	
Chunk	Divide the text into parts.	
Compact	Make each chunk smaller.	
Conceptualize	Think of a keyword for each chunk.	
Connect	Combine the keywords into a summary sentence.	

Source: Adapted from McEwan-Adkins (2010), *40 Reading Intervention Strategies for K-6 Students*

Another time students may need structured support is when you are asking them to make inferences or higher-level analyses. Again, providing a graphic organizer with specific prompts to help them organize their thoughts is helpful.

Analyzing a Text	
What facts are in the article, story, or book?	
What are points the author implies, but doesn't directly state?	
How do your real-life experiences help you understand what the author is saying?	
What have you read or heard in school that will help you understand what the author is saying?	

You can stop after this organizer, moving to a class discussion. Or, you may want students to write a detailed analysis. If so, they can move to another set of organizing questions.

Organizer for Analysis		
Fact One from Text	Fact Two from Text	Fact Three from Text
Inference Related to Fact	Inference Related to Fact	Inference Related to Fact

When writing your analysis, it's important to state the inferences you made, supported by the evidence you have gained from the facts. You may also include your real-life experiences and other insights you have learned in school.

Key Point/Inference One	Key Point/Inference Two
Evidence	Evidence
Overall Key Point(s) of Analysis	

By chunking the information visually, students are better prepared to write a narrative analyzing text.

Structured Modeling

Structured modeling is also needed when you expect students to complete a process, a higher-order task, or a project. This often occurs when you ask students to answer questions or complete a project that requires more than just reciting facts, such as describing the causes of an event in history, persuading the reader of a position, or explaining how to solve a math problem. Each type of question requires higher-level thinking skills and applying all those facts they memorized.

Chances are, your at-risk students don't do well with these types of questions or similar assignments such as reports or projects. Again, don't assume that it's because they don't want to or just aren't doing it. Many students simply don't know how to do this correctly. As teachers, it is our job to activate or provide background knowledge with content, as well as process. Let's look at a framework for making performance expectations explicit with higher-level assignments. In our case, we'll look at asking students to write an extended response, or essay-type answer.

Start by discussing the assignment with students: "One task you'll need to complete to be successful in my class is to answer essay questions appropriately. How many of you have written answers to essay questions before?" "What did you have to do to make a good grade on them?" Discuss the answers, clarifying misconceptions. Most of the time, you don't grade based on the number of sentences; that may reflect depth, but many times it doesn't.

Second, show a sample of a *good or acceptable* answer to a question. Be sure to tell students this is an example you would consider to be good. Have students read the sample or read it with them. Discuss what you are looking for in an answer. It's important that your expectations are clear. Before this class, decide on your key criteria for what makes a good answer, and state those in terms that are understandable to students.

Discuss what you are looking for: "Just as there are discipline rules in a school to ensure order and acceptable behavior, there are basic procedures to follow to be successful with learning. First, you need to answer the question. Sometimes students will put in extra information that doesn't answer the question, because they think they need more words or sentences. That can actually make your answer worse." Continue to describe other rules. "Just as a reminder, for the first few weeks of school, I will post the procedures." Show the poster on your wall that lists the criteria and provides visual reinforcement.

Third, gently discuss the differences between your procedures and their experiences. Don't tell your students they are wrong; explain that you want them to understand what they need to do to be successful in your class: "You'll notice that my rules are a little different from what you told me you did last year. Although you can't really answer my questions with just a sentence or two, I don't just count the number of words or sentences. I look at whether you actually answered the question, whether or not you gave at least three examples to support your answer, and so on. I know this may be a little different, so let's see what that actually looks like." Show a sample answer on the board, the overhead, or in a handout; and point out exactly how the sample meets your expectations. Be sure to give specific examples.

Fourth, give students another sample answer, preferably on a handout. Pair students and have them read the answer and decide whether or not it follows the rules. You might even have them guess the grade, but I usually start just with satisfactory or not satisfactory rather than A, B, or C. Lead a whole-class discussion, going to each of your rules and asking students whether or not the sample meets the rule and why or why not: "Let's talk about how this answer matches the criteria. The first guideline is that a question should answer the question. The question was [insert sample here]. Does this answer actually answer that?" Students respond. "Can you tell me where exactly in the essay it answers the question?" Again, allow students to respond.

Fifth, using the same process, provide a second example to give students another chance to practice looking for good responses. As they write their own answers, explain that they need to do the same things. If students are hung up on particular misconceptions such as always needing three paragraphs, give them a model that does so but is bad in other ways so they can see the difference in criteria.

Sixth, give them a question to answer, reminding them that they should complete the answer using your rules. Pick a simple question; your focus in this lesson is on the process of writing a good answer rather than demonstrating they understand new content. That is ultimately your desired result, but let's do the basics first. Remember, if students don't know where they want to go (a good response), they also don't know how to walk (how to get there).

Finally, have them either write down the guidelines from your poster or give them a writer's checklist to use as they complete their short essay. During the next lesson or the next day, review the rules with your students through an interactive discussion. As you go through each rule, ask them to look at their own essays to check if they followed the rule. Have them physically check each rule on the paper or the checklist. Then pair them up again to check each other's papers, again rule by rule, while you move around the room monitoring their work. Give them the chance to rewrite their answers before they turn them in for a grade.

This process is effective with any process you use with your students. Working through this process takes several days and may need to be revisited throughout the year. Also, the use of rubrics supports this process. Providing students with a clear set of clarifying statements for each criterion on your procedures chart can help them improve their writing throughout the year.

Understanding Is the Result

Effective support always results in a deeper understanding of the content rather than memorization of facts. As I learned, if a student does not understand decimals, more practice doesn't help. We need to find different ways to present the information so that students internalize what they are learning.

Christy Matkovich points out that teachers must find a way to deliver information to students "so their brains learn it. It might be drawing a picture or through movement. If your form of delivery isn't working, then find a different way to deliver it." Ideally, your lesson should include enough options for each student to learn in his or her own way. But if some students don't learn, then it's up to you to find a new way to help them understand.

Sometimes the best help comes from another student rather than the teacher. As Shannon Knowles explains, "I regularly have one student who understands explain the concepts to those who don't. Sometimes, they explain to everyone in class, sometimes to the one or two who need it. They just say it in a way that makes more sense to the students."

In her book, *Social Studies Worksheets Don't Grow Dendrites* (2012), Marcia L. Tate gives an example of teaching interpretation skills for understanding. She suggests using posters to study events or periods in history (sources include the National Archives or the Library of Congress).

However, just using the posters is not particularly effective with struggling learners. They don't necessarily know what to look for. So she recommends using guided observations to understand the posters.

Observations

- What are the main colors used?
- What symbols, if any, are used?
- Are the symbols clear, memorable, and/or dramatic?
- What is the message in the poster?
- Who created the poster? (government, special interest groups, a for-profit company, and so forth)
- Who is the intended audience for the poster?
- What response was the creator of the poster hoping to achieve?
- What purpose does the poster serve?

All of these strategies have one thing in common: they use information to guide students to a higher level of understanding.

Provides for Differentiation

Good support also provides for some differentiation. Now, that doesn't mean I think you need to provide 32 different scaffolding activities for 32 different students. There are times that an individual student needs individual scaffolding. But for many of our struggling learners, they need similar help, so you can provide ways to help them within your normal lesson.

For example, vocabulary is a huge struggle for students. No matter what you teach, students are expected to learn specialized vocabulary for your subject. And because words have multiple meaning in different subjects, it can be confusing.

One way to provide support with vocabulary is to create personalized dictionaries. Give each student a file folder. If you'd like, have them decorate the front cover with pictures and words related to the topic or story you are reading. As you teach a lesson, ask them to write the key vocabulary on post-it notes, and place the stickies in their folders in alphabetical order.

Throughout the lesson, they add to their folders. For example, if they read an article and find related words, they add more sticky notes. If your class discussion brings in a new word, add a sticky note (those would be for everyone). By the end of the unit, each one has a personalized dictionary. Since you have made these with file folders, they can collect multiple ones to create a larger dictionary, either customized to your subject, such as science, or for a collection of stories or literature.

A second strategy I particularly like also uses post-it notes. We'll look at a basic version of the strategy that is particularly pertinent for younger students, then an adaptation for older ones.

Choose pictures from magazines or newspapers (you can use a variety, or center all your pictures around a theme or topic). Paste the pictures on the front of a folder. Have students in small groups (four or five maximum) look at the picture and individually write words that describe the picture on small post-it notes (one word per note). Use a time limit of 2–3 minutes, depending on your group.

Next, have the group work together to put their words in categories that are similar (you can use nouns/verbs/adjectives, or some other way of categorizing words based on the standards and objectives of the lesson). If you are teaching language arts, this is a great opportunity to teach some grammar skills.

The group then uses their notes to build a sentence describing the picture. They will need to use additional post-its to add articles and needed punctuation. Ask groups to share their sentences and pictures, and lead a short discussion of expressive writing. Next, have the students individually write paragraphs.

Typically struggling students are stuck at this point, unsure how to begin. However, they have the sentence the group built to use as a starting point. Usually, my students then started asking me how to spell words, or what words to use. In this case, you can point them back to the group work. Every group will have extra sticky notes they didn't use. In essence, the groups built customized word banks, which is an excellent resource for your struggling learners.

Notice how this is an activity that can be used with all learners to write a descriptive paragraph. But the support is built into the activity for those learners that need it. Now, what if you want to do a more advanced version of the activity with older students?

In this case, choose pictures from news or magazine stories (be sure to save the accompanying story). Have students in small groups (four or five maximum) look at the picture and individually write words that describe the picture on small post-it notes (one word per note). Use a time limit of 2–3 minutes, depending on your group.

Again, have the group work together to put their words in categories that are similar (you can use nouns/verbs/adjectives, or some other way of categorizing words based on the standards and objectives of the lesson).

The group then uses their notes to build a sentence describing the picture. They will need to use additional post-its to add articles and needed punctuation. Next, have them open the folder. Inside is the accompanying article. Have the students look at the headline of the accompanying story. Using a K-W-L chart, have each group write what they already THINK they know about the story, using the headline and the picture.

Ask members of the groups to read the article. Compare and contrast the accuracy of the original sentence with the actual story—did the sentence written from the picture agree with the story? Did it accurately reflect the story? Did it add additional details, etc.? Again, the comparison and contrast can be tailored to meet your specific standards and objectives. You may also adapt the writing assignment to meet the specific subject you are teaching. For example, I observed a secondary science classroom that used pictures of varying planets, along with accompanying information. It was interesting to notice the need for observational skills while working with the pictures.

Promotes Connections

We also want to provide support that promotes connected learning. When students are able to connect new learning with what they already know or what they are learning in other subjects, it is more effective. We always want to link the unfamiliar with something familiar. The majority of new concepts we teach can be learned, but only in relation to other concepts.

I visited one school that emphasized learning prefixes and suffixes in the English/Language Arts classrooms. But the students were just memorizing the meanings. Struggling students in particular didn't do well, because they didn't understand how prefixes and suffixes related to anything else. The teachers created a bulletin board that was divided into four parts. There was a circle in the center with the prefix or suffix, and the four sections were labeled math, science, social studies, and everything else.

Students looked for examples of words that used the prefix/suffix in all their other classes. Teachers were careful to use them whenever possible. Then, the English/Language Arts teacher led discussions of the applicability of the prefix or suffix. Although everyone benefited, the teachers saw an increase in learning among struggling students because they were able to make connections.

Another way to help students make connections is through similes, metaphors, and analogies. At the early grades, this can begin with simple comparisons. Marcia L. Tate, in *Social Studies Worksheets Don't Grow Dendrites*, shares an example. She recommends using the book *I'm as Quick as a Cricket* by Audrey Wood as a prompt for similes. Once you read the books to and with your students, ask them to fill in the pattern, *I'm as _____ as a _____*. Then discuss those similes and how the students made the connections.

For older students, she recommends asking them to form direct analogies by taking one concept and connecting it to another concept that is dissimilar. For example, *How is democracy like a railway station?* Or *How is an election like a pizza?* Not only are you teaching connections, it encourages students to become critical thinkers.

Finally, you always want to encourage students to connect their learning to three other types of concepts: their own experiences, something they have learned in school, and something in real-life. We used this process in the analysis example in the Structured Support section earlier in the chapter, but here's a simple graphic organizer you can use with students throughout your lessons.

New Concept		
How it relates to me	How it relates to something else I've learned	How it relates to real-life

Optimizes Strategic Learning

In Chapter 7: Engagement, I mentioned that there are two types of prior knowledge—content knowledge and strategic knowledge. Many of our students can't focus on the content when they don't understand the strategy they should use for learning. We need to help them optimize their strategic knowledge in order to be motivated to learn.

One strategy that many students struggle with is that of taking notes. And, as teachers, we may assume students know how to take notes. Too often, students either write down everything they see or hear, or they write nothing down. Unfortunately, neither is effective.

Today, we often use PowerPoint or Prezi to put notes up on a screen. However, students simply copy the PowerPoint. This isn't note-taking; again, this is copying. It's important to teach students the strategy of taking notes. Although this may take time, you will reap the benefits later. I recommend the following 10-step process.

> **Steps for Teaching Note-Taking**
> 1. Discuss the importance of taking notes.
> 2. Point out that taking notes is writing some of what is written or said.
> 3. Use a PowerPoint slide to show a section of text.
> 4. Model identifying three to five key words or phrases to write down.
> 5. Demonstrate how to write additional notes or an explanation without looking at the screen.
> 6. Ask students to do the next screen on their own.
> 7. Provide additional modeling and guided practice as needed.
> 8. Ask students to practice note-taking during a lesson.
> 9. Provide feedback as to the quality of the notes.
> 10. Remind students as needed of the appropriate way to take notes.

You may be thinking this isn't practical for you; it sounds like a tremendous amount of work to teach something your students should be able to do before they come to your class. I know I thought my students should be able to take notes when I was teaching upper elementary students.

Our choice is to complain or help our students learn. The time investment pays off with an overall increased quality of responses. Ideally, you should do this at the beginning of the school year; but if you are in the middle of the school year, don't put off trying this strategy for another year. Better late than never. It really is simple: Define what you are looking for, explain it to your students, and show them examples. Too often, we are so busy covering the content, we forget to do the basics of the strategic process.

Repetitionless

In one of my workshops, a teacher said, "I know how to provide help for my students. Help means extra practice. The more help they need, the more homework I assign." That is not effective support. Repetition only works for memorizing isolated facts, and even that only provides short-term learning. Repetition rarely provides long-term learning.

As Christy Matkovich says, "Practice needs to be quality. If the day didn't go well, if my students are lost or confused, then we'll just go home and start over the next day. If I send homework on a day like that, they'll create a way to do it, then we have to unlearn!" It's harder to "unteach" bad learning than it is to invest extra time in making sure that your students truly understand.

If I don't understand something, practicing it over and over again isn't going to help. Hearing it again, told to me in the same words, only slower or louder, isn't going to help. It's important for students to practice what they are learning in a variety of ways. Look for opportunities for them to hear about the lesson, talk about their learning, write about their learning, and do something with their learning. By practicing from a variety of angles, the understanding is more likely to stick with a student.

Jason Womack, a former high school teacher, shares the structure for his class periods. Each day the first task for students was to copy the schedule off the board. He organized his instruction around a theme for the day and always listed 5 to 12 activities. Typically, he scheduled 10, 5-minute activities. He wanted students to see, hear, and touch something at least twice every day. In a typical day, they would

> see something (watch me or data); hear about it (listen to me lecture or use the closed-eye process [tell 4–7 min. story with eyes closed]) . . . touch something (come back from wherever they went to [in their mind] and produce something based on what they heard: draw, write it, make a video, . . . or a puppet show). My goal was to give them information and let them internalize and give it back; not just force-feed info and make them regurgitate it, but to give them an opportunity to internalize and express it.

He also ensured that his students truly understood the concepts he was teaching.

Tied to Memory

Finally, effective support must be tied to a student's memory. We touched on part of this in the Promotes Connections section earlier in the chapter, but I want to expand on how important this is. Francis Bailey and Ken Pransky, in their book *Memory at Work in the Classroom: Strategies to Help Underachieving Students*, point out that our semantic memory is like a computer hard drive in our heads. It's where we store all our memories and it's the foundation of academic learning. When new concepts are stored in semantic memory, they are not only interconnected, but they are stored in a way to represent relationships among concepts.

Schemas are representations of learning in an interconnected way. Schemas can incorporate concepts, propositions, symbols, facts, frames, or scripts. How does this apply to learning? Let's look at examples of each of those provided by Bailey and Pransky.

Schema	Example
Concepts	themes in literature or the distributive property
Propositions	democracy is the best form of government
Symbols	ABC, $, Π
Facts	3 × 4 = 12, Mt. Everest is 29,028 feet high
Frames	a rectangle has four square angles, two sets of parallel lines, and opposite sides of equal length
Scripts	visit to the dentist, solving a two-step math problem, inferring the meaning of a word from context

Source: Bailey and Pransky (2014), *Memory at Work in the Classroom: Strategies to Help Underachieving Students*

Consider each of these examples of schemas. If you'll notice, there are varying levels of higher-order thinking. For example, scripts require more thinking than facts. But in order for any of these to stay in a person's long-term memory, it must be taught in a way that connects it to what a student already knows.

Judy Willis, a neurologist and classroom teacher, also provides us insight into helping students store information in their memory. She provides eight tips we can apply in our classrooms.

Notice how many of her suggestions relate to concepts we've already discussed. Helping students tie new learning to their memory so they can readily access the information is the result of providing effective support.

Conclusion

Struggling learners need additional support as they learn. When they don't feel successful, they aren't motivated to learn, so we should provide scaffolding to help ensure their success. Effective support is structured, leads to understanding, provides for differentiation, promotes connections, optimizes strategic learning, limits repetition, and is tied to memory. The final result: student understanding.

Points to Ponder

Use the following sentence starters to reflect on the chapter.

I learned . . .
I'd like to try . . .
I need . . .
I'd like to share something from this chapter with . . .

9

Resilience

Introduction

Winston Churchill once said, "Success is not final, failure is not fatal: It is the courage to continue that counts." That's really what resilience is about. Resilience is that "something" that helps us deal effectively with pressure, to bounce back from failure and to address and positively overcome everyday challenges.

In *Building Resilience in Children and Teens*, Kenneth Ginsburg (2011) points out there are seven "crucial C's" of resilience: competence, confidence, connection, character, contribution, coping, and control. Think of these as a braided cord, with each strand interwoven with the others. The more of them you have, the stronger you are.

For example, when you feel competent, that typically builds confidence, which gives you a sense of control, which in turn, helps you cope. Each is important, but together, they make you stronger. Part of motivating struggling students is fostering resilience in them. We'll look at three areas related to resilience.

Areas Related to Resilience
Characteristics of Teachers Who Encourage Resilience
Views of Failure
Grit

Characteristics of Teachers Who Encourage Resilience

You may be asking yourself, "Aren't these character traits? Do I really have any influence in these areas?" You absolutely can make a difference. These characteristics are learned—whether at home, from their friends, or at school. There are specific actions you can take to positively impact resilience in your struggling students.

You must start with your beliefs about resilience. You have a choice—believe you can make a difference or that you can't—whichever you think will happen. Resilience isn't constant in our lives; you've probably had periods of time you were more, or less, resilient. The same is true of our students. Just as we discussed in Chapter 6: High Expectations, your beliefs may come out in surprising ways. Watch out for thoughts like "He's just not good at that." or "She's at risk. That's probably the best she can do."

We also need to be sure that we view our struggling students as individuals who do have strengths and hopes, rather than as problems that must be solved. That perspective enables us to treat them as gifts to be nurtured and treasured rather than something to be bothered with.

10 Strategies for Raising Resilient Students

Robert Brooks and Sam Goldstein (2001) in *Raising Resilient Children*, provides 10 guideposts for teachers (and parents) who foster resilience. Here are the 10 strategies, and we'll look at each in turn.

---

10 Strategies for Raising Resilient Students

1. Being empathetic
2. Communicating effectively and listening actively
3. Changing "negative scripts"
4. Loving our children in ways that help them to feel special and appreciated
5. Accepting our children for who they are and helping them to set realistic expectations and goals
6. Helping our children experience success by identifying and reinforcing their "islands of competence"
7. Helping children recognize that mistakes are experiences from which to learn
8. Developing responsibility, compassion, and a social conscience by providing children with opportunities to contribute
9. Teaching our children to solve problems and make decisions
10. Disciplining in a way that promotes self-discipline and self-worth

---

1. Being Empathetic

As we discussed in Chapter 2: Building a Relationship, it's important that we care about our students. But we also need to move beyond the surface to truly understand who they are and how they feel.

I had a student who was a constant challenge, and I taught him for 2 ½ years! Todd came into my class with a reputation as an at-risk learner, and in seventh grade he lived up to it. By the eighth grade, he was trying to improve, but he struggled to move beyond his past patterns and others' preconceived notions of him. The turning point in our student-teacher relationship came when I discovered he had a talent for drawing, and I arranged for him to do some artwork for a special project. I was amazed at the turnaround from a completely negative attitude in my class the prior year to a positive attitude. He used his art to help him process learning. In fact, if other students were struggling, he would share his drawings with them to help them understand.

I'm always reminded of Todd's story when I read my favorite children's book, *The Phantom Tollbooth* by Norton Juster. During their journey, Milo, Tock, and the Humbug end up jumping to the Island of Conclusions, which turns out to be a less-than-pleasant place. I jumped to conclusions about Todd based on our first day of class together, and it took me 2 years to move past that and build a strong relationship. I regret the wasted time, because I could have made so much more progress with him if I had started our teacher-student learning relationship differently. Making the choice to *not* jump to conclusions is less about our students than it is about who we are as teachers.

"Now will you tell me where we are?" asked Tock as he looked around the desolate island. "To be sure," said Canby; "you're on the Island of Conclusions. Make yourself at home. You're apt to be here for some time." "But how did we get here?" asked Milo, who was still a bit puzzled by being there at all. "You jumped, of course," explained Canby. "That's the way most everyone gets here. It's really quite simple; every time you decide something without having a good reason, you jump to Conclusions whether you like it or not. It's such an easy trip to make that I've been here hundreds of times." "But this is such an unpleasant-looking place," Milo remarked. "Yes, that's true," admitted Canby; "it does look much better from a distance."

Source: Norton Juster (1988), *The Phantom Tollbooth*

---

2. Communicating Effectively and Listening Actively

One way we show empathy is by communicating effectively with our struggling learners, and that includes truly listening to them. A teacher in one of my workshops shared with me that she always tried to take time for her students, especially when there were breaks between classes or activities. As you might imagine, she also had other responsibilities, so she typically scanned the room while talking to students, just to make sure everything else was running smoothly.

One day, a student was asking her a question, and the student suddenly became quiet. When the teacher asked what was wrong, the student said, "You weren't paying attention to me. You're paying attention to everyone else." The teacher immediately stopped, looked her in the eye, and said, "What do you want to say?" She began to listen actively as opposed to multitasking. That's important to students.

We also need to make sure we are communicating clearly. There are four keys to effective communication:

1. fully answer the question being asked;
2. provide clear information;
3. be positive in your word use; and
4. finish with a question or a next step the person should take.

By following these principles, my students understood me better, and it improved our relationship.

3. Changing "Negative Scripts"

Students who are not resilient typically have a negative script running in their heads at all times. In their minds, they hear comments like, "You're no good." or "You shouldn't have tried." It's important for us, as teachers, to address this with our struggling students, and help them reframe the negatives as positives.

Negative Script	*Positive Script*
You can't do anything right. You aren't any good at math. Why do you even bother trying? I just want to quit!	Everyone makes some mistakes. The important thing is to learn from them. Math may be a struggle right now, but you can do it with help from your teacher and some effort. Everyone has to try sometimes. And lots of famous people tried many times before they succeeded. I can keep trying until I get there. Success is about putting in the effort.

Be sure to actively model reframing negative scripts into positive ones, and help your students do the same.

4. Loving Our Children in Ways That Help Them to Feel Special and Appreciated

In Chapter 3: Praise and Positive Feedback, we talked about how to focus on the positives with students. We don't need to revisit that information, but let me reinforce how important it is to individualize our attention to students so that it helps them feel special.

It's important to consider the emphasis on "ways that help them to feel special and appreciated." It's not just what we think; it's what makes them feel that way. Whether you are praising a student or encouraging him or her, think about what makes each one unique. Some want to be noticed for behavior, others for academics, still others for just being who they are. There are students who prefer to be noticed in public ways; others in a more private manner. Know them well enough to make them feel like the unique personalities they are.

5. Accepting Our Children for Who They Are and Helping Them to Set Realistic Expectations and Goals

Are you beginning to see how resilience ties in with everything else we've discussed? We talked about goal setting in Chapter 4: Empowerment and Ownership, and we looked at realistic expectations in Chapter 6: High Expectations.

In this context, however, I want to point out that accepting students for who they are does not mean simply allowing them to stay where they are in the learning process. You can accept a student and still have high expectations for them to grow. The caution, however, is that we push them so hard we inadvertently send a message that they aren't "good enough."

There is a balance between helping them achieve more and accepting them. My niece, Asheland, is 8 years old. Her mother and I both have dreams for her future. We imagine all sorts of wonderful opportunities for her, some of which she hasn't even dreamed of herself. Does that mean we don't love her now? No. We accept her with all her talents, but encourage her to spread her wings. That's what we want to do with all our struggling students.

6. Helping Our Children Experience Success by Identifying and Reinforcing Their "Islands of Competence"

Too often, struggling students don't recognize their own strengths. In order to help them build their confidence, which produces a willingness to try new things, we must help them identify their strengths.

You can do this naturally as you teach. Notice what a student is doing well, comment on it, and reinforce it. But you may also want to do a "strengths inventory," a simple assessment that helps you identify and summarize students' strengths.

Strengths Inventory	
Academics	*Motivation*
___Has strong prior knowledge ___Participates in class ___Seeks opportunities to learn	___Is intrinsically motivated ___Motivated by school and learning ___Responds to extrinsic motivation
Organization	*Type of Work*
___Is organized ___Has good work habits ___Completes work	___Works well independently ___Works well with a partner ___Works well in groups
Social Skills	*Emotional Skills*
___Has variety of friends ___Demonstrates empathy ___Cares about others	___Can control emotions ___Accepts responsibility ___Has positive self-esteem

7. Helping Children Recognize That Mistakes Are Experiences from Which to Learn

Too often, students who are not resilient give up because they see even the slightest mistake as a permanent failure and a sign that they should stop trying. Working with this perspective is so important, I'm going to spend an entire section on it later in this chapter.

For now, let's look at an example of how to teach struggling students that making mistakes is a normal part of the learning process.

Robert Brooks and Sam Goldstein (2001) share:

One elementary school teacher told her class on the first day of school that throughout the year they would celebrate mistakes. She humorously explained that if her students did not make mistakes, she might lose her job, since it would mean that they already knew everything she had to teach them. She placed a glass jar on her desk with a box of stones and told them, "whenever you or I make a mistake, someone will come up and drop a stone into the jar.

As soon as the jar is filled, I will bring in the popcorn for celebration." Apparently the jar was small enough and the stones large enough that the party always took place within the first week. Students who typically would not raise their hands for fear of making a mistake now volunteered to answer; after all, if their answer was incorrect, they would be helping the class move one step closer to celebration.

8. Developing Responsibility, Compassion, and a Social Conscience by Providing Children with Opportunities to Contribute

Too often, we are so focused on standardized testing and academic achievement that we overlook skills such as responsibility, compassion, and a social conscience. Although these can be characteristics that describe a person, they are learned skills.

We help students develop these by building in opportunities for them to contribute to the classroom and the larger community. For example, assigning students different tasks within the classroom is an excellent way to develop responsibility.

Students can also develop empathy for others when we provide opportunities for collaboration. One strategy I used in my classroom was to group students with different strengths together. Then, they could capitalize on the gifts each one had. I remember one year, students were working on a major project. Andrew, one of my brightest students became very frustrated. He shouted, "I just don't know what to do with this!" Another student in the group, one who struggled and would be considered an at-risk student, immediately grabbed the materials and started showing him how to build the model.

Andrew was upset because he couldn't see the big picture. Although a strong academic student, the project required creativity and thinking out of the box, which wasn't his strong suit. The "struggling" student, though, was much more apt to take a broader view of topics, and quickly spotted how to complete the project. Throughout this process, Andrew developed more empathy for students who didn't necessarily get the right answer immediately. Providing opportunities for students to coach each other is a good way to develop empathy.

Finally, projects that are tied to the larger community can help students gain a social conscience. I was in a school recently where students planted a garden, and developed a piece of equipment for capturing rainwater to nurture the garden. Many other schools have student-designed recycling programs. There are many ways to tie academics to service projects.

9. Teaching Our Children How to Solve Problems and Make Decisions

It's a natural part of any classroom for students to solve problems. We use problem-solving all the time in math, but we can incorporate this strategy in every subject.

For example, you can do something as simple as allowing students to choose 5 out of 10 questions to answer. Or select a story or novel from a recommended book list and justify their choice. By allowing choices, you are providing an easy introductory strategy to problem solving.

The use of graphic organizers is particularly helpful. For example, I've been in many classrooms that use a problem-solution graphic to help students organize their thinking. This sample is used in elementary reading classrooms to identify the problems and solutions for the beginning, middle, and end of a story.

Organizer for Analysis		
Beginning	*Middle*	*End*
Problem	Problem	Problem
Solution	Solution	Solution

You may also want to teach students a formal process for problem solving. In the following middle school/secondary example, students work

Problem Solving with a Scientific Inquiry

What are you testing?	• Create a testable question. • Test one variable.
Research topic information	• Key fact 1 • Key fact 2 • Key fact 3
State hypothesis	• What is a predicted answer to your question? • What may be the possible outcome of the investigation?
Design an experiment	• Control all variables except the independent variable. • Plan for independent and dependent variables with repeated trials. • Plan for factors that should be constant. • Plan for a control set-up. • List materials needed to conduct your experiment. • List procedures you will follow to conduct your experiment. • Record your data. • Organize your data. • Analyze your data.

through the process of scientific inquiry (South Carolina Science Curriculum Standards Support Guide 7–1.3).

10. Disciplining in a Way That Promotes Self-Discipline and Self-Worth

Finally, we must consider how we discipline our students. There are two approaches to discipline: one that is focused on order and punishment and one that involves students and promotes student self-discipline. Richard Curwin, Allen Mendler, and Brian Mendler in *Discipline with Dignity* (2008) provide multiple recommendations. Several are particularly pertinent for our purposes.

1. Build a strong relationship with your students.
2. Make sure students are never the butt of your jokes.
3. Refuse to accept excuses for their behavior (and don't make excuses for them).
4. Legitimize misbehavior that you cannot stop (for example, if students like to talk to each other, provide 2 minutes at the end of class for them to chat).
5. Allow students to take responsibility for themselves.
6. Start fresh every day.

These strategies provide guidance as we find ways to discipline students in positive ways.

Views of Failure

Earlier, I mentioned that one way to help students build resilience is to help them recognize that mistakes help you learn. How students view mistakes reflects how they feel about failure. For example, we all know people who have made a mistake or failed in some way, learned a lesson, and later became successful.

Two People Who Have Overcome Failure

Steve Jobs

You always hear about a "long road to the top," but perseverance isn't limited to the early stages of a person's career. Oftentimes, failure can occur after a long period of success.

Steve Jobs achieved great success at a young age. When he was 20 years old, Jobs started Apple in his parents' garage, and within a decade the company blossomed into a $2 billion empire. However, at age 30, Apple's Board of Directors decided to take the business in a different direction, and Jobs was fired from the company he created. Jobs found himself unemployed, but treated it as a freedom rather than a curse. In fact, he later said that getting fired from Apple was the best thing to ever happen to him, because it allowed him to think more creatively and re-experience the joys of starting a company.

Jobs went on to found NeXT, a software company, and Pixar, the company that produces animated movies such as *Finding Nemo*. NeXT was subsequently purchased by Apple. Not only did Jobs go back to his former company, but he helped launch Apple's current resurgence in popularity. Jobs claimed that his career success and his strong relationship with his family were both results of his termination from Apple.

J.K. Rowling

J.K. Rowling, author of the *Harry Potter* books, is currently the second-richest female entertainer on the planet, behind Oprah. However, when Rowling wrote the first *Harry Potter* book in 1995, twelve different publishers rejected it. Even Bloomsbury, the small publishing house that finally purchased Rowling's manuscript, told the author to "get a day job."

At the time when Rowling was writing the original *Harry Potter* book, her life was a self-described mess. She was going through a divorce and living in a tiny flat with her daughter. Rowling was surviving on government subsidies, and her mother had just passed

---

away from multiple sclerosis. J. K. turned these negatives into a positive by devoting most of her free time to the *Harry Potter* series. She also drew from her bad personal experiences when writing. The result is a brand name currently worth nearly $15 billion.

Source: Excerpt from www.growthink.com/content/7-entrepreneurs-whose-perseverance-will-inspire-you

According to UC Berkeley professor Martin Covington (in Zakrewski, 2014), students generally fall into four categories as to how they cope with failure. See if you recognize any of your students in the descriptions.

Success-Oriented Students	*Overstrivers*
These are the kids who love learning for the sake of learning and see failure as a way to improve their ability rather than a slight on their value as a human being. Research has also found that these students tend to have parents who praise success and rarely, if ever, reprimand failure.	These students are what Covington calls the "closet-achievers." They avoid failure by succeeding—but only with herculean effort motivated solely by the fear that even one failure will confirm their greatest fear: that they're not perfect. Because the fear of failure is so overpowering and because they doubt their abilities, Overstrivers will, on occasion, tell everyone that they have very little time to prepare for an upcoming test—and then spend the entire night studying. When they pass the test with flying colors, this "shows" everyone that they are brilliant because their "ability" trumped the need to extend any effort.
Failure-Avoiding	*Failure-Accepting*
These students don't expect to succeed—they just want to avoid failing. They believe that if they extend a lot of effort but still fail, then this implies low ability	These are the hardest students to motivate because they've internalized failure—they believe their repeated failures are due to lack of ability

(continued)

and hence, low worth. But if they don't try and still fail, this will not reflect negatively on their ability and their worth remains intact.

In order to avoid failure that might be due to lack of ability, they do things such as make excuses (the dog ate my homework), procrastinate, don't participate, and choose near-impossible tasks. However, this can put them into a tricky position when they encounter a teacher who rewards effort and punishes for what appears to be lack of effort or worse. Ultimately, there's no way out for these students—either they try and fail or they're punished.

and have given up on trying to succeed and thus maintain their self-worth. Any success they might experience they ascribe to circumstances outside their control such as the teacher giving them the easiest task in a group project.

It's important to help students learn to deal with failure in a positive manner. There are four steps you can take to do so.

1. Remind them of others (famous people, people from literature, local role models) who have failed, but later succeeded.
2. Share your own stories of what you have learned from mistakes, as well as telling stories (anonymously) of other students who have been successful.
3. Treat each mistake as a learning opportunity. Focus on the positive and how students can grow in the future.
4. Constantly and consistently reinforce that mistakes and failures are a natural part of learning. After all, if your students already knew everything, they wouldn't need you!

There are also specific strategies you can use with the four types of students.

Student Type	Strategies
Success-Oriented	Continue to support and encourage their efforts
Overstriver	Reinforce that effort is just as, or more important than ability, using real-life examples. Positively reinforce the effort they do put forth; deemphasize grades.
Failure-Avoiding	Provide opportunities with guaranteed success. Chunk projects so they can complete small steps without being overwhelmed by the big picture. Remind them of past successes, which will build confidence.
Failure-Accepting	Provide valid (not too easy so as to be perceived as "dumbed down") opportunities with guaranteed success. Chunk projects so they can complete small steps along with extra support and scaffolding to help them succeed. Consistently reinforce what they are doing right, and praise their efforts.

Social Emotional Learning (SEL)

Another concept related to resilience is that of social emotional learning, or the process through which children and adults acquire and effectively apply the knowledge, attitudes, and skills necessary to understand and manage emotions, set and achieve positive goals, feel and show empathy for others, establish and maintain positive relationships, and make responsible decisions (Collaborative for Academic, Social, and Emotional Learning, n.d.).

Carla Tantillo Philibert, author of *Everyday SEL*, describes a mindful practices SEL framework.

Mindful Practices SEL Framework	
Component	*Description*
Self-awareness	Self-esteem, body awareness, personal responsibility, developing emotional awareness and understanding choice.
Self-regulation	Adaptability, expressing emotions, managing stress and anxiety, problem solving, coping skills and decision-making skills.
Social-awareness	Active listening, empathy, service orientation and community building.
Social-regulation	Leadership, managing vulnerability, collaboration, teamwork, influence of self and others, relationship with self and others, peer-to-peer communication.

Source: From Carla Tantillo Philibert. Used with permission.

Some struggling students have strong social and emotional skills, but others do not. Therefore, we need to actively teach social and emotional strategies to those who need them. Tantillo Philibert once again provides suggestions.

Strategies for Teaching the Four Components

Component	*Strategies*
	(Note: To begin, implement once or twice, 3–5 minutes a day to shift frenetic student energy to calm, focused energy. Whole class implementation is preferred with extended time for students with exceptionalities.)

Self-awareness: Practicing these activities will help students move from powerlessness to self-control.	**Getting to Know My Emotions and Feelings** Using stories, fables, photos, news articles, and "real-life" examples, introduce students to different emotions such as Sad, Joyful, Angry, Frustrated, Fearful, Excited, Anxious, and/or different feelings such as Hungry, Calm, Focused, Relaxed, Tired, Stressed, Vulnerable, Shameful, and Hurt (physical vs. emotional)
Self-regulation: Practicing these activities will help students move from impulsivity to navigating choices around their behavior.	**Write & Rip:** Students record (write or draw) negative feelings, experiences, and emotions on a sheet of scrap paper. After writing for a set amount of time (4 minutes on average) the students rip up their paper and toss it in the recycling bin, effectively "letting go" of negativity to help them be more centered and less reactive.
Social-awareness: Practicing these activities will help students move from a reactive to a more communal view of the world.	**Shoulder Share:** Students sit shoulder-to-shoulder, facing opposite directions. The teacher gives the students a talking prompt such as *How Can We Improve Our Behavior After Lunch?* or, *Preparing for the Big Test Tomorrow.* Upon the teacher's cue, one student shares his/her thoughts. The other student simply listens, he/she does not comment or critique his/her partner's thoughts. After a set amount of time (1.5 minutes on average) the students switch who is speaking and who is listening. When the activity concludes, the teacher may/may not cue the students to share depending on the topic.
Social-regulation: Practicing these activities will help students move from feeling disconnected to the world around them to feeling like a valued and contributing member of their peer group.	**Compliment Circle:** Students stand in 2 concentric circles facing each other, so that each student is standing across from a peer. The teacher prompts the students to share a time that the other student was exhibiting positive behavior such as being kind, compassionate, caring, joyful, fun, creative, etc. Each student has 1 minute to share before the circle rotates to find new sets of partners. (For this to be successful, it is important the teacher appropriately frame the activity by discussing the difference between a true, observational compliment and a joke or self-deprecating comment.)

Source: Tantillo Philibert. Used with permission.

Grit

A final topic within the concept of resilience is grit. Many students have grit, just not in terms of academics. Grit is perseverance: the decision (and ability) to keep moving forward rather than giving up. When we are teaching grit, students may experience some frustration. That is normal; in fact, if they aren't experiencing frustration, then they do not have the opportunity to use grit.

Students who demonstrate grit are more confident, and ultimately, learn at higher levels. Therefore, it is important for us to teach and reinforce this skill. How can we do that? There are two basic steps.

Two Steps for Teaching Grit
1. Create a climate that encourages grit.
2. Provide opportunities for students to demonstrate grit.

Create a Climate That Encourages Grit

Your first step is to make sure your overall classroom environment encourages grit. This starts with you! Share your own experiences where you struggled and persevered. Model it for students. I remember one year when I was teaching graduate students. They were all teachers coming to school at night to work on a master's degree. Research writing was a challenge for them. One night, I brought in an article I had written for a journal, one that had been rejected.

I showed them the comments, and then explained what I was going to do to revise and resubmit the article. It was an eye-opener for them. As Kim said, "I never realized you didn't write perfectly all the time!" Our students don't see us struggle. They think we just magically do what we do. It's important to show them otherwise.

We can also provide role models with stories of people who have persevered. This can be with posters of those people along with a quote exemplifying how they overcame success, or by reading about them. One strategy I used was to have my students research someone who struggled and create the posters with accompanying narrative. Today, I would probably have them create a fake Facebook page on a poster for display.

Another alternative is to use literature to learn about perseverance. Of course, you can read non-fiction books and articles, but there are also examples in literature that teach this lesson.

Young Adult Novels That Teach Grit	
Sonia Nazario	*Enrique's Journey*
Pam Mynoz Ryan	*Experanza Rising*
Gary Paulsen	*Hatchet*
Sharon Draper	*Out of My Mind*
Chris Crutcher	*Ironman*
Mildred D. Taylor	*Roll of Thunder, Hear My Cry*
Suzanne Collins	*The Hunger Games*
Timothee de Formbelle	*Toby and the Secrets of the Tree*
Lawrence Yep	*Dragonwings*

Children's Literature That Teaches Grit	
Watty Piper	*The Little Engine That Could*
Mary Hoffman	*Amazing Grace*
Patricia Polacco	*Thank You, Mr. Falker*
Tommie de Paola	*The Art Lesson*
Patty Lovell	*Stand Tall, Molly Lou Melon*
Dr. Seuss	*Horton Hatches an Egg*
Matt Whitlock	*Gigantic Little Hero*
Spike Lee, Tonya Lewis Lee, and Sean Qualls	*Giant Steps to Change the World*
Pat Thomas and Lesley Harker	*I Can Do It! A First Look at Not Giving Up*

Third, talk about grit. Be explicit when discussing the role of grit in learning. Regularly use words such as frustration, tenacity, perseverance, resilience, and self-confidence. Also be sure to praise students specifically using this vocabulary when their efforts warrant it.

Provide Opportunities for Students to Demonstrate Grit

The second step is to allow students to actually practice using grit. This one is a bit tricky. You must know your students well enough to know how much frustration they can handle, and then provide them a learning opportunity in which they will struggle. Quick success is not your goal in crafting the activity; providing them an opportunity to feel frustrated and respond is.

Thomas Hoerr (2013) describes an effective process to use when presenting students a learning opportunity to develop grit.

1. Create frustration
   a. Before they start, ask students to anticipate how hard the assignment might be and to think about something else they have done at the same level.
   b. Next, ask them to think about a task when they were successful and how grit played a role.
   c. Then, have students work on the assignment with 5 minutes of full force effort. When they struggle, they should stop and breathe, reflect, and try something else.
   d. Remind students that a good failure is one where you learn. What are you learning?
2. Monitor the experience
   a. Gauge how frustrated they are using a simple scale (numbers or just up and down).
   b. Ask how they respond to frustration. Place them in groups based on the strategies they used for a response. Ask the groups to discuss.
   c. Create a checklist to monitor progress. You may want something like a two-column chart with headings of key points in the lesson on the left and a place for notes on the right. For younger students, you can keep this as the teacher (based on your observations); for older students, they can self-assess.
3. Reflect and learn. Discuss the lessons learned. Then celebrate progress!

Take care with the amount of "grit opportunities" you provide. For many of your struggling learners, everything is a "grit opportunity." These, however, will be structured experiences in which you coach them as to how to respond appropriately. You'll also want to make sure they understand what you are doing and why so they don't give up.

Conclusion

Resilience is the ability to effectively handle pressure and to overcome failure. It is a characteristic that many of our struggling students do not have in the classroom; yet it is one that we can teach. By being empathetic; communicating effectively and listening actively; changing "negative scripts"; loving our children in ways that help them to feel special and appreciated; accepting our children for who they are and helping them to set realistic expectations and goals; helping our children experience success by identifying and reinforcing their "islands of competence"; helping children recognize that mistakes are experiences from which to learn; developing responsibility, compassion, and a social conscience by providing children with opportunities to contribute; teaching our children to solve problems and make decisions; and disciplining in a way that promotes self-discipline and self-worth, we can help our students learn to overcome failure, develop grit, and truly become resilient.

Points to Ponder

Use the following sentence starters to reflect on the chapter.

I learned . . .
I'd like to try . . .
I need . . .
I'd like to share something from this chapter with . . .

10

Celebrating Diverse Groups of Students

Introduction

Many Pathways of Learning

One child may see . . .

Even a young child with a gift for visual thinking might draw pictures well and use line, shape and colour to communicate ideas. Drawing, painting, diagramming, mapping might be the ways that this child expresses herself best. Showing her pictures or charts may be a good way to help her learn.

One child may dance . . .

Some children (and adults) learn by moving. Such a child might learn dance steps in a few seconds, or express himself as a mimic or clown. This child might learn about the solar system, for example, by moving through a "planet dance."

One child may face a special obstacle . . .

A child might have an injury that keeps him from holding chalk or a pencil. Another might have poor hearing that keeps her from participating in class, or even from saying words properly. As teachers, we can take notice of students who face special challenges, and find ways to help them. We can use our creativity to make our classes vital and filled with opportunities for all learners.

Source: UNICEF, www.unicef.org/teachers/learner/paths.htm

Do you believe this quote from UNICEF? Do you think you can use your creativity to make your class full of opportunities for *all* your learners? Our classrooms today are filled with diversity. The question is not will it ever get better. The question is, do you view diversity as a deficit or as a design?

One of my most cherished possessions is a quilt from my grandmother, who passed away many years ago. She collected scraps for many years, but before she died, she sewed the scraps together in a beautiful design. I believe that's what diversity in our classroom is like. You have students who come from impoverished homes, who are gifted, who have attention deficit disorder, or who may be culturally diverse. Are you willing to use your teaching skills to weave your students together in a beautiful classroom quilt?

In this chapter, we're summing up by looking at ways to work with specific groups of students. Keep in mind that I have not included every possible diverse group of students, just those that are typically found in today's classrooms. And, in a sense, we're painting with a broad brush; I'm providing a quick overview of different types of challenges we face in the classroom. We'll look at 10 specific groups.

Diverse Groups of Students

Gifted Students
Underachievers
Culturally Diverse Students
At-Risk Students
Students from Poverty
Students with Learning Disabilities
Students with Autism
Students with Attention Deficit Disorder
English Language Learners

Gifted Students

You may be thinking, "This is a book about struggling students. Why is she writing about gifted learners?" I find that gifted students can also struggle, particularly when they are bored, they are uninterested, or they perceive that the teacher or their peers are less than competent. What are some tips for working with gifted students to keep them from struggling? Julia Thompson (2013) provides assistance.

10 Tips for Teaching Gifted Students

1. Give reasonably loose structure to allow them to take the project as far as they need to.
2. Allow them a strong voice in how they will accomplish their goals. Recognize their self-direction.
3. Set a rapid pace for instruction.
4. Focus on having students use higher-level thinking skills, as they quickly master (and are bored by) recall and comprehension questions.
5. Use technology as often as you can.
6. Provide content that challenges them and matches their interests.
7. Encourage student input in the selection of materials. Ask them to synthesize information from a variety of sources.
8. Don't ask gifted students just to solve problems, have them use real-life situations to formulate their own problems.
9. Focus on depth of content rather than quantity.
10. Whenever possible, move instruction out of the classroom so that students can study material firsthand.

Underachievers

Do you teach any underachievers? These are students who have the potential to achieve at high levels, but they never reach that potential. Their parents are often highly successful, and are very involved in their children's lives. Students who are underachievers use elaborate defense mechanisms to protect themselves from the anxiety of failing. It's often easier to give up, or not try at all, than it is to try and fail. Once again, Thompson provides us some tips for working with this group of students.

Working with Underachievers

1. Accept that these students' shortcomings are not the result of laziness, even though they may see themselves as lazy and worthless.
2. Work with parents, but be aware that overinvolvement can sometimes increase a student's anxiety.
3. Strive to make assignments so appealing that all students will want to do them. Underachievers need extra motivation. They seldom find the work intrinsically interesting.
4. Don't expect your underachieving students to be more than briefly motivated by their own success.
5. Work out a plan to guarantee that work will be turned in on time. Underachievers often do not turn in work even when they have completed it.
6. Use a checklist of steps to accomplish the assignment.
7. Teach study skills, time management, and organization strategies.
8. Be matter of fact about assignments. Don't show emotion or frustration.
9. Be positive and supportive.
10. Be aware that underachievers seldom ask for help. Be proactive in offering assistance.
11. Offer frequent and unobtrusive encouragement to help them move past their perfectionist approach.
12. Don't accept excuses such as, "I'm just lazy" or "I never do well in math."

Culturally Diverse Students

Several years ago, a teacher shared with me a story about her students. She explained that many of her students came from a culturally diverse background, and, in particular, did not understand the difference between using formal language and slang language in the classroom.

One day, she brought two items with her to class: a swimsuit and a black dress. She asked her students where she should wear the swimsuit. She then explained she would be attending a funeral the next day; should she wear the swimsuit there? The students immediately responded, "No. You should wear the dress." She used that example to explain the difference between using formal language and more expressive slang. There's a place for each, but you have to pick and choose your times.

I thought that was an excellent example of dealing with cultural diversity. Too often, we simply reprimand students for something that is their culture, rather than trying to bridge the gap. That's why I like the culture boxes described in Chapter 2: Building a Relationship. They help you understand where your students are coming from.

The first step to working with students from cultural diversity is to discover your own biases. Linda Ross (n.d.) gives us some guiding questions.

Self-Quiz: What Are Your Assumptions?

Ask Yourself . . .

- What are the different cultures in my school? (Include categories such as various ethnic groups, students with disabilities, new immigrants, residents of public housing, and any other relevant groupings.)
- What characteristics first come to mind when I think of each group?
- Where did these impressions come from? (Peers, family, media, religion, etc.) How reliable are these sources?
- How do I treat people based on these impressions?
- Can I remember a time when someone made assumptions about me based on a group I belong to? How did it make me feel?

Next, consider how culture affects behavior. Ross continues by describing various ways this occurs.

How Culture Affects Behavior

1. **Speaking Up:** Sociologists draw a distinction between high-context societies in which there are many rules and people say less, and low-context societies that depend on explicit verbal messages.
2. **Tracking Time:** There are also different cultural takes on time: monochronic, meaning that people do one thing at a time and adhere to schedules, and polychronic, in which people do several things at a time, put interpersonal needs over schedules, and may view time as an invasion of self.
3. **Physical Self:** Culture shapes the kinds of gestures we use for example, beckoning someone is offensive in some cultures and the amount of personal space we need to feel comfortable.
4. **Personal Interaction:** Importantly for teachers, our cultures also contribute to how we view cooperation, competition, and discipline.

Finally, be sure you are responding appropriately to the different cultures of your students. For example, in some cultures relationships are more important than information. Therefore, when you meet with parents (and with your students), you must build a relationship before you share information.

Take a moment to look at your walls and the teaching materials you use. Do they represent the diversity of your students? If you have Latino or Hispanic students, are there posters on your wall of role models who look like them? If you teach African American students, are they represented in your textbooks and other reading materials? We can't just spend one day on a culture and say we are responding to our students. We must integrate their cultures into our instruction.

At-Risk Students

Students may be at-risk for a number of reasons, including poor skills, drugs or alcohol problems, pregnancy, emotional issues, family concerns, illness, or homelessness. Although some of these strategies are applicable to all students, they are particularly pertinent for those at-risk.

Working with At-Risk Students

1. Be persistent in efforts to motivate.
2. Spend time helping them establish life goals so they can see a purpose for staying in school.
3. Set small goals.
4. Involve students in cooperative learning activities to connect them to other students.
5. Invite guest speakers or older students to talk about the importance of staying in school.
6. Be generous with praise and attention.
7. Check on them when they are absent.
8. Provide opportunities for success.
9. Offer extra help and assistance.
10. Connect to them in positive ways to show you care.

Source: Thompson (2013), *The First-Year Teacher's Survival Guide*

Students from Poverty

It is important when working with students from a poverty background to not make assumptions. Oftentimes, they do not have the background knowledge other students have. For example, my husband and I had a foster son for several months. Prior to his time with us, he had been homeless, and he grew up in poverty. The first time we took him to a restaurant, he didn't know how to use cloth napkins and he was stunned at the concept of leaving a tip.

When I was teaching, the majority of my students lived in poverty. However, I grew up in a middle-class household. I didn't fully understand their circumstances or perspective. For example, when they didn't do their homework, it was often because they didn't have the resources at home. I would have provided the resources, but they didn't tell me. After all, who wants to admit they don't have paper or pencils at home?

It's important to acknowledge that your students who live in poverty are different; they are members of a group that has specific needs. Because they don't have resources at home, they may never have learned how to organize materials. If their parents aren't educated, education may not be reinforced. They may or may not have positive role models in their lives. Recognizing these facets of your students helps you be more empathetic and more willing to help meet their specific needs.

One may make the assumption that students who come to school with expensive sneakers and clean clothes would also come to school with the appropriate school supplies such as paper and a pencil or pen. Value is placed on different items with students in poverty. It is not that they cannot afford a pencil or paper. It is more important to come to school and appear "normal" and look and act like other students. Parents will invest in clothes and shoes for their children rather than materials for school. Students in poverty may also have the appropriate materials, yet they will not keep up with them because they are of less value than other materials such as clothes and shoes.

Students with Learning Disabilities

Approximately 3 percent to 6 percent of all school-age children and adolescents are believed to have developmental reading disabilities. In fact, almost 50 percent of children receiving special education have learning disabilities.

Key Statistics

The overall dropout rate for students without disabilities is approximately 11% (U.S. Department of Education, 2001).
"Students with emotional/behavioral disorders have a dropout rate between 50% and 59% while between 32% and 36% of students with learning disabilities drop out of school" (Kemp, 2006, 236).
"More than 60% of prison inmates have learning disabilities" (Pitt, 2003).

While these statistics seem frightening, they are a reminder that we need to work harder and smarter early in children's lives and sustain our efforts to make a long-term effect. Additionally, a critical fact remains: just because a student is labeled learning disabled or at risk, it does not mean he or she is incapable of learning. Students with learning disabilities have average to above-average intelligence. Therefore, ensuring their success in school is a matter of finding the appropriate teaching strategies and motivation tools, all of which we can control as teachers.

So, we can make a difference with students with learning disabilities. According to the Learning Disability Association of America, there are three intervention practices that produce positive outcomes:

- ◆ direct instruction;
- ◆ learning strategy instruction; and
- ◆ using a sequential, simultaneous structured multi-sensory approach.

What does that look like in the classroom? The Association describes eight specific actions teachers can take to make a difference.

Eight Specific Actions

1. break learning into small steps;
2. administer probes;
3. supply regular, quality feedback;
4. use diagrams, graphics and pictures to augment what they say in words;
5. provide ample independent, well-designed intensive practice;
6. model instructional practices that they want students to follow;
7. provide prompts of strategies to use; and
8. engage students in process type questions like "How is the strategy working? Where else might you apply it?"

Students with Autism

Who exactly are students with autism? There are stereotypes that abound, but autism is a part of many teachers' lives through the students they teach. In many cases, students with high-functioning autism are in the regular classroom. What is autism? WebMD provides the following medical definition.

Autism is a brain disorder in which communication and interaction with others are difficult. The symptoms of autism may range from total lack of communication with others to difficulty in understanding others' feelings. Because of the range of symptoms, this condition is now called autism spectrum disorder (ASD). High-functioning autism (HFA) is at one end of the ASD spectrum. Signs and symptoms are less severe than with other forms of autism. In fact, a person with high-functioning autism usually has average or above-average intelligence.

Then, how do we work with students who have autism, particularly if they are high-functioning? The Georgia Department of Education provides guidelines.

---

15 Tips for Teaching High-Functioning Students with Autism

1. People with autism have trouble with organizational skills, regardless of their intelligence and/or age. Always praise the student when he remembers something he has previously forgotten. Never denigrate or "harp" at him when he fails. Attempt to train him in organizational skills using small, specific steps.
2. People with autism have problems with abstract and conceptual thinking. Be as concrete as possible in all your interactions with these students.
3. An increase in unusual or difficult behaviors probably indicates an increase in stress. Sometimes stress is caused by feeling a loss of control. Many times the stress will only be alleviated when the student physically removes himself from the stressful event or situation.
4. Do not take misbehavior personally. The high-functioning person with autism is not a manipulative, scheming person who is trying to make life difficult. They are seldom, if ever, capable of being manipulative. Usually misbehavior is the result of efforts to survive experiences which may be confusing, disorienting, or frightening.
5. Use and interpret speech literally. Until you know the capabilities of the individual, you should avoid:
   ♦ Idioms
   ♦ Double meanings
   ♦ Sarcasm
   ♦ Nicknames
   ♦ "Cute" names (Pal, Buddy)
6. Remember that facial expressions and other social cues may not work. Most individuals with autism have difficulty reading facial expressions and interpreting "body language."
7. If the student doesn't seem to be learning a task, break it down into smaller steps, or present the task in several ways (e.g., visually, verbally, physically).
8. Avoid verbal overload. Be clear. Use shorter sentences.
9. Prepare the student for all environmental and/or changes in routine. Use a visual or written schedule to prepare him for change.
10. Behavior management works, but if incorrectly used it can encourage robot-like behavior, provide only short-term behavior

(continued)

change, or result in some form of aggression. Use positive and chronologically age-appropriate behavior procedures.

11. Consistent treatment and expectations from everyone is vital.

12. Normal levels of auditory and visual input can be perceived by the student as too much or too little. For example, the hum of florescent lighting is extremely distracting for some people with autism. Consider environmental changes such as removing "visual clutter" from the room or seating changes if the student seems distracted or upset by his classroom environment.

13. If your high-functioning student with autism uses repetitive verbal arguments and/or repetitive verbal questions, you need to interrupt what can become a continuing, repetitive litany. Continually responding in a logical manner or arguing back seldom stops this behavior. Try requesting that he write down the question or argumentative statement. This usually begins to calm him down and stops the repetitive activity. Then write down your reply.

14. If your class involves pairing off or choosing partners, either draw numbers or use some other arbitrary means of pairing. These students could benefit most from having a partner.

15. Assume nothing when assessing skills. For example, the individual with autism may be a "math whiz" in Algebra, but not able to make simple change at a cash register. Or, he may have an incredible memory about books he has read, speeches he has heard or sports statistics, but still may not be able to remember to bring a pencil to class. Uneven skills development is a hallmark of autism.

Students with Attention Deficit Disorder

Attention deficit hyperactivity disorder (ADHD) is a disorder that appears in young children. You may know it by the name *attention deficit disorder*, or ADD. ADD/ADHD makes it difficult for people to inhibit their spontaneous responses, whether that is verbally or physically. Not every child has ADD/ADHD, but if a child shows symptoms across all environments, it is important to consider. You likely have a student with ADD/ADHD in your classroom. What specific strategies are helpful for him or her?

Strategies for Working with ADD/ADHD Students

Teach school success skills (such as taking notes or following directions).

Clearly define classroom procedures.

Monitor them unobtrusively by placing them near you.

Give them extra assistance during transition times.

Give directions one step at a time.

Give students copies of particularly difficult text with key parts highlighted.

Offer alternative auditory modes of learning.

Encourage computer use.

Review frequently.

Source: Thompson (2013), *The First-Year Teacher's Survival Guide*

English Language Learners

Finally, let's consider English Language Learners, students who do not have English as their native language. In *Diverse Learners in the Mainstream Classroom*, Yvonne and David Freeman and Reynaldo Ramirez explain that there are very specific ways to help these students learn in the classroom. Remember, in addition to learning your content, they are still struggling to learn the language, so lessons are a particular challenge.

Strategies for Working with English Language Learners

1. Draw on students' first languages to preview and review the lesson.
2. Use visuals and realia.
3. Scaffold content learning through the use of graphic organizers.
4. Use gestures and body language.
5. Speak clearly and pause often, but don't slow down speech unnaturally.
6. Paraphrase regularly.
7. Write key words and ideas down.
8. Use media when appropriate.
9. Make frequent comprehension checks.
10. Keep oral presentations and reading assignments short. Collaborative activities are more effective than lectures or assigned readings.

Conclusion

Motivating struggling learners includes working with diverse groups of students, ranging from those who are just learning to speak the language to those who are gifted. Each group has unique characteristics, but there are strategies you can use to make a difference; it truly depends on whether you want to take the time to best meet their needs.

As we finish our book, I want to remind you that you do make a difference for students every day, even when you don't feel like it. A friend of mine, Sam Myers, is a coordinator of an alternative school for students who are not successful in the regular school setting. He greets his teachers every morning by saying, "On your worst day, you are someone's best hope." I like that, but I don't quite agree.

I believe that on your worst day, you are not someone's best hope. On the day that you spilled coffee on your shirt, and your son missed the bus, and you were late to work, and the copier was broken, and you came into your classroom filled with students who each had a burning question for you, you are not someone's best hope. You are, for at least one student in your classroom, their *only hope*. My hope for you is that you remember that.

Points to Ponder

Use the following sentence starters to reflect on the chapter.

I learned . . .
I'd like to try . . .
I need . . .
I'd like to share something from this chapter with . . .

Bibliography

ADD / ADHD in Children. (n.d.). Signs and symptoms of Attention Deficit Disorder in kids. Retrieved December 23, 2014 from http://www.helpguide.org/articles/add-adhd/attention-deficit-disorder-adhd-in-children.htm

Ames, R. & Ames, C. (1990) "Motivation and effective teaching." In B. F. Jones and L. Idol (eds.), *Dimensions of thinking and cognitive instruction.* Hillsdale, NJ: Erlbaum.

Azzam, A. M. (2014, September). Motivated to learn: A conversation with Daniel Pink. *Educational Leadership, 72*(1): 12–17.

Bailey, F. & Pransky, K. (2014). *Memory at work in the classroom: Strategies to help underachieving students.* Alexandria, VA: Association for Supervision and Curriculum Development.

Blackburn, B. R. (2005). *Classroom motivation from A to Z: How to engage your students in learning.* New York: Routledge.

Blackburn, B. R. (2007). *Classroom instruction from A to Z: How to promote student learning.* New York: Routledge.

Blackburn, B. R. (2008). *Literacy from A to Z: Engaging students in reading, writing, speaking, & listening.* New York: Routledge.

Blackburn, B. R. (2012a). *Rigor made easy.* New York: Routledge.

Blackburn, B. R. (2012b). *Rigor is not a four-letter word, 2nd edition.* New York: Routledge.

Blackburn, B. (2014). *Rigor in your classroom: A toolkit for teachers.* New York: Routledge.

Blackburn, B. & Witzel, B. (2013). *Rigor for students with special needs.* New York: Routledge.

Brooks, R. & Goldstein, S. (2001). *Raising resilient children.* New York: McGraw-Hill.

Chapman, C. & Vagle, N. (2011). *Motivating students: 25 strategies to light the fire of engagement.* Bloomington, IN: Solution Tree Press.

Chauncey, T. & Walser, N., eds. (2009). *Spotlight on student engagement, motivation, and achievement.* Cambridge, MA: Harvard Education Press.

Coe, R., Aloisi, C., Higgins, S., & Major, L. (2014, October 1). What makes great teaching? Review of the underpinning research. Retrieved November 3, 2014, from http://www.suttontrust.com/wp-content/uploads/2014/10/What-makes-great-teaching-FINAL-4.11.14.pdf

Collaborative for Academic, Social, and Emotional Learning. (n.d.). What is Social Emotional Learning? Retrieved January 15, 2015 from http://www.casel.org/social-and-emotional-learning/

Conklin, W. (2006). *Instructional strategies for diverse learners*. Huntington Beach, CA: Shell Education.

Covington, M. (2009). "Self-worth theory: Retrospection and prospects." In K. Wentzel & A. Wigfield (eds.), *Handbook of motivation at school* (pp. 141–169). New York, NY: Routledge.

Csikszentmihaly, M. (2004). *Flow: The psychology of optimal experience*. New York: Harper.

Curwin, R. L. (2010). *Meeting students where they live: Motivation in urban schools*. Alexandria, VA: Association of Supervision and Curriculum Development.

Curwin, R. L. (2014, September). Can assessments motivate? *Educational Leadership, 72*(1): 38–40.

Curwin, R., Mendler, A., & Mendler, B. (2008). Discipline with dignity. Alexandria, VA: Association of Supervision and Curriculum Development.

Dinkmeyer, D. & Losoncy, L., eds. (1992). *The encouragement book*. New York: Simon and Schuster.

Dweck, C. (2007). *Mindset: The psychology of success*. New York: Ballantine Books.

Dweck, C. S. & Elliott, E. S. (1983). "Achievement motivation." In P. Mussen & E. M. Hetherington (eds.), *Handbook of child psychology* (pp. 643–691). New York, NY: Wiley.

Edmondson, E. (2012). Wiki literature circles: Creating digital learning communities. *English Journal, 101.4*: 43–49.

Education Week Research Center. (2014). *Engaging students for success: Findings from a national survey*. Washington DC: Author.

Eubank, T. (n.d.). *Instant credit recovery or instant "content" recovery for middle grades: ICR summary and implementation strategies* (unpublished whitepaper). Southern Regional Education Board. Accessed January 3, 2011.

Ferlazzo, L. (2011). *Helping students motivate themselves: Practical answers to classroom challenges*. New York: Routledge.

Ferlazzo, L. (2012, October 15). Response: Classroom strategies to foster a growth mindset. Retrieved September 12, 2014, from http://blogs.edweek.org/teachers/classroom_qa_with_larry_ferlazzo/2012/10/response_classroom_strategies_to_foster_a_growth_mindset.html?qs=caroldweck

Ferlazzo, L. (2013). *Self-driven learning: Teaching strategies for student motivation*. New York: Routledge.

Florida Department of Education. (n.d.). *Strategies that enhance setting high expectations for all students*. Office of School Improvement Information Ways Series Number Five. Florida: Author.

Freeman, Y. S., Freeman, D. E. & Ramirez, R., eds. (2008). *Diverse learners in the mainstream classroom*. Portsmouth, NH: Heinemann.

Gambrell, L. (1996). Creating classrooms cultures that foster reading motivation. *The Reading Teacher, 50*: 4–25.

Gardner, H. (1983). *Frames of mind: The theory of multiple intelligences.* New York: Basic Books.

Gerstein, J. (n.d.). How educators can assist learners in developing a growth mindset. Retrieved May 12, 2014, from https://usergeneratededuca-tion.wordpress.com/2014/09/28/how-educators-can-assist-learners-in-developing-a-growth-mindset/

Gibbons, P. (2015). *Scaffolding language scaffolding learning.* 2nd edition. Portsmouth, NH: Heinemann.

Gibbs, G. (1994). *Learning in teams: A student manual.* Oxford: Oxford Brookes University.

Ginsberg, M. B. & Wlodkowski, R. J. (2000). *Creating highly motivating classrooms for all students: A schoolwide approach to powerful teaching with diverse learners.* San Francisco, CA: Jossey-Bass.

Ginsburg, K. R. (2011). *Building resilience in children and teens: Giving kids roots and wings.* 2nd edition (with M. M. Jablow). Elk Grove Village, IL: American Academy of Pediatrics.

Goleman, D. (2005). *Emotional intelligence: Why it can matter more than IQ.* New York: Bantam Books.

Goleman, D. (2007). *Social intelligence: The new science of human relationships.* New York: Bantam Books.

Goodwin, B. & Miller, K. (2013, September 1). Research says / Grit plus talent equals student success. Retrieved September 12, 2014, from http://www.ascd.org/publications/educational-leadership/sept13/vol71/num01/Grit-Plus-Talent-Equals-Student-Success.aspx

Green, R. L. (2014). *Expect the most: Provide the best.* New York: Scholastic.

Harris, B. (2012, July 18). Building resiliency in struggling students. Retrieved January 5, 2014.

Hattie, J. & Yates, G. (2008). *Visible learning: A synthesis of over 800 meta-analyses relating to achievement.* New York: Routledge Taylor & Francis Group.

Hattie, J. & Yates, G. (2014). *Visible learning and the science of how we learn.* New York: Routledge Taylor & Francis Group.

High-Functioning Autism and Asperger's Syndrome. (n.d.). Retrieved January 12, 2015, from http://www.webmd.com/brain/autism/high-functioning-autism

Hoerr, T. R. (2013). *Fostering grit.* Alexandria, VA: Association of Supervision and Curriculum Development.

How to make growth-mindset theory work in the classroom. (2014, January 11) Retrieved January 12, 2014, from http://news.tes.co.uk/b/tes-professional/2014/10/31/how-to-make-growth-mindset-theory-work-in-the-classroom.aspx

Jackson, R. R. (2011). *How to motivate reluctant learners.* Alexandria, VA: Association of Supervision and Curriculum Development.

Jakes, T. D. (2014). *Instinct: The power to unleash your inborn drive.* Brentwood, TN: FaithWords Publishing.

Jensen, E. (2003). *Tools for engagement: Managing emotional states for learner success*. Thousand Oaks, CA: Corwin Press.

Jensen, E. (2013). *Engaging students with poverty in mind: Practical strategies for raising achievement*. Alexandria, VA: Association of Supervision and Curriculum Development.

Juster, N. (1988). *The phantom tollbooth*. New York: Random House.

Keller, S. (2012, April 26). Increase your team's motivation five-fold. *Harvard Business Review*. Retrieved October 5, 2014 from http://blogs.hbr.org/cs/2012/04/increase_your_teams_motivation.html

Kemp, S. E. (2006). Dropout policies and trends for students with and without disabilities. *Adolescence, 41* (162), 235–250.

Kohn, A. (1999). *Punished by rewards*. Boston: Houghton Mifflin.

Kohn, A. (2000). *Hooked on rewards*. Parents Magazine.

Lavoie, R. (2007). *The Motivation Breakthrough: Six secrets to turning on the tuned-out child*. New York: Touchstone.

Many Pathways of Learning. (n.d.). Retrieved December 12, 2014, from http://www.unicef.org/teachers/learner/paths.htm

Marzano, R. J. (2004). *Building background knowledge for academic achievement: Research on what works in schools*. Alexandria, VA: Association for Supervision and Curriculum Development.

Marzano, R. J. (2010, September). High expectations for all. *Educational Leadership, 68*(1): 82–84.

Marzano, R. J., Pickering, D. J. & Pollock, J. E. (2001). *Classroom instruction that works*. Alexandria, VA: Association for Supervision and Curriculum Development.

Maslow, A. (1943). A theory of human motivation. *Psychological Review*.

McEwan-Adkins, E. K. (2010). *40 reading intervention strategies for K-6 students*. Bloomington, IN: Solution Tree Press.

McInnes, A. (2011, June 13). Give your colleagues three compliments for every criticism. Retrieved October 5, 2014 from http://blogs.forrester.com/andrew_mcinnes/11-06-13 give_your_colleagues_three_compliments_for_every_criticism

Merrell, K. W. & Gueldneer, B. A. (2010). *Social and emotional learning in the classroom: Promoting mental health and academic success*. New York: The Guilford Press.

Michalko, M. (2006). *Thinkertoys: A handbook of creative thinking techniques*. Berkeley, CA: Ten Speed Press.

Middleton, M. & Perks, K. (2014). *Motivation to learn: Transforming classroom culture to support student achievement*. Thousand Oaks, CA: Corwin Press.

O'Brien, A. (2011, October 5). *Bullying prevention: 5 tips for teachers, principals, and parents*. Retrieved November 4, 2014 from http://www.edutopia.org/blog/bullying-prevention-tips-teachers-parents-anne-obrien

Opitz, M. F. & Ford, M. P. (2014) *Engaging minds in the classroom: The surprising power of joy*. Alexandria, VA: The Association for Supervision and Curriculum Development.

O'Quinn, P., ed. (2013). *Instructional strategies that work*. San Francisco, CA: Julian John Publishing.

Paideia active learning. (2015). Retrieved January 12, 2015 from http://www.paideia.org

Peters, S. G. (2008). *Teaching to capture and inspire all learners: Bringing your best stuff every day!* Thousand Oaks, CA: Corwin Press.

Pink, D. H. (2011). *Drive: The surprising truth about what motivates us*. New York: Riverhead Books.

Pitt, T. (2003, November 18). Charles Schwab didn't let dyslexia stop him. *USA Today*. Retrieved from http://usatoday30.usatoday.com/money/companies/management/2003-11-10-schwab_x.htm

Quate, S. & McDermott, J. (2009). *Clock watchers*. Portsmouth, NH: Heinemann.

Quate, S. & McDermott, J. (2013). *The just-right challenge: Nine strategies to ensure adolescents don't drop out of the game*. Portsmouth, NH: Heinemann.

Quate, S. & McDermott, J. (2014, September). The just-right challenge. *Educational Leadership, 72*(1): 61–65.

Rattan, A., Good, C. & Dweck, C. (2012). It's okay, not everyone can be good at math: Instructors with an entity theory comfort (and demotivate) students. *Journal of Experimental Social Psychology*.

Reeves, D. (2007). *Ahead of the curve: The power of assessment to transform teaching and learning*. Bloomington, IN: Solution Tree.

Ricci, M. C. (2013). *Mindsets in the classroom*. Waco, TX: Prufrock Press, Inc.

Rollins, S. P. (2014). *Learning in the fast lane: Eight ways to put all students on the road to academic success*. Alexandria, VA: Association for Supervision and Curriculum Development.

Roscoria, T. (2014, November 10). 5 ways schools can make learning relevant for students. Retrieved December 10, 2014, from http://www.centerdigitaled.com/news/5-Ways-Schools-Can-Make-Learning-Relevant-for-Students-.html

Ross, L. (n.d.). Connect with kids and parents of different cultures: How to develop positive relationships with today's diverse families. Retrieved January 12, 2015, from http://www.scholastic.com/teachers/article/connect-kids-and-parents-different-cultures-0

Schlechty, P. (2011). *Engaging students: The next level of working on the work*. San Francisco, CA: Jossey-Bass.

Settle, S. A., & Milich, R. (1999). Social persistence following failure in boys and girls with LD. *Journal of Learning Disabilities, 32*: 201–212.

17 Tips For Teaching High Functioning Students with Autism. (n.d.). Retrieved January 12, 2015, from http://www.gadoe.org/Curriculum-Instruction-and-Assessment/Special-Education-Services/Documents/IDEAS 13 Handouts/17 Tips For Teaching High Functioning People with Autism.pdf

Southern Regional Education Board. (2004). *Ten strategies for creating a classroom culture of high expectations*. http://publications.sreb.org/2004/04v03_Ten_Strategies.pdf. Atlanta, GA: Author.

Stipek, D. (n.d.). How do teachers' expectations affect student learning. Retrieved March 3, 2014, from http://www.education.com/reference/article/teachers-expectations-affect-learning/

Successful Strategies for Teaching Students with Learning Disabilities. (n.d.). Retrieved January 12, 2015, from http://ldaamerica.org/successful-strategies-for-teaching-students-with-learning-disabilities/

Sullo, B. (2007). *Activating the desire to learn*. Alexandria, VA: Association for Supervision and Curriculum Development.

Tantillo, C. (forthcoming). *Everyday social emotional learning*. New York: Routledge Publishing.

Tate, M. L. (2012). *Social studies worksheets don't grow dendrites*. Thousand Oaks, CA: Corwin Press.

Teacher Praise: An Efficient Tool to Motivate Students. (n.d.). Retrieved March 3, 2014, from http://www.interventioncentral.org/behavioral-interventions/motivation/teacher-praise-efficient-tool-motivate-students

Thompson, J. G. (2013). *The first-year teacher's survival guide*. San Francisco, CA: Jossey-Bass.

Tileston, D. W. (2010). *What every teacher should know about student motivation*. 2nd edition. Thousand Oaks, CA: Corwin Press.

21 Simple Ideas to Improve Student Motivation. (2012, December 10). Retrieved March 3, 2014, from http://www.teachthought.com/teaching/21-simple-ideas-to-improve-student-motivatio/

27 Ways To Promote Intrinsic Motivation In The Classroom. (n.d.). Retrieved September 12, 2014, from http://www.teachthought.com/teaching/27-ways-promote-intrinsic-motivation-classroom/

U.S. Department of Education, National Center for Education Statistics. (2001). *Dropout rates in the United States: 2000*, NCES 2002-114. Washington, DC: Author.

Vygotsky. L. S. (1978). *Mind in society*. Cambridge, MA: Harvard University Press.

What Is Social and Emotional Learning. (n.d.). Retrieved January 15, 2015 from http://www.casel.org/social-and-emotional-learning/

Wiederhold, C. (1995). *Cooperative learning and higher level thinking: The Q-matrix*. San Clemente, CA: Kagan.

Williamson, R. & Blackburn, B. (2010). *Rigorous schools and classrooms: Leading the way*. New York: Routledge.

Williamson, R. & Blackburn, B. (2011). *Rigor in your school: A toolkit for leaders*. New York: Routledge.

Willis, J. (2006). *Research-based strategies to ignite student learning*. Alexandria, VA: Association for Supervision and Curriculum Development.

Witzel, B. S. (2007). Using contingent praise to engage students in inclusive classrooms. *Teachers as Leaders, 7*: 27–32.

Witzel, B. S. & Mercer, C. D. (2003). Applying rewards to teach students with disabilities: Implications for motivation. *Remedial and Special Education, 24*: 88–96. Thousand Oaks, CA: Sage.

Wormeli, R. (2014, September). Motivating young adolescents. *Educational Leadership, 72*(1): 26–31.

Wright, C. (2013, September 12). Three pillars for supporting resilience. Retrieved November 5, 2014, from http://www.ascd.org/ ascd-express/vol8/825-wright.aspx?utm_source=ascdexpress&utm_ medium=email&utm_campaign=express825

Zakrewski, V. (2014, March 7). How to help kids overcome fear of failure. Retrieved September 5, 2014, from http://www.huffingtonpost.com/ vicki-zakrzewski-phd/how-to-help-kids-overcome_b_4915497.html